Creative Interventions
for
Bereaved Children

Liana Lowenstein

Champion Press
Toronto

Printed in Canada by Hignell Book Printing.

Library and Archives Canada Cataloguing in Publication

Lowenstein, Liana, 1965-
     Creative interventions for bereaved children / Liana Lowenstein.

Includes bibliographical references.
ISBN 0-9685199-2-X

1. Bereavement in children. 2. Children and death. 3. Children-Counseling of.
4. Child psychotherapy. 5. Group counseling for children. I. Title.

BF723.G75L682006   155.9'37083   C2006-902983-0

Correspondence regarding this book can be sent to:
Liana Lowenstein c/o Champion Press
Pharma Plus, PO Box 91012, 2901 Bayview Avenue, Toronto, Ontario, Canada M2K 1H0
Telephone: 416-575-7836 Fax: 416-756-7201
Email: liana@globalserve.net Web: lianalowenstein.com

Acknowledgments

I am ever so grateful to the many children and families who, during my years of clinical practice, have moved and enlightened me. The bereaved children hold a special place in my heart, because my mother died during my childhood. To them, I extend my deepest gratitude for helping me to make meaning of my loss, and for reminding me that something good can come from tragedy. I dedicate this book to my bereaved clients. May your pain be transformed into wisdom, strength, and compassion.

My sincere appreciation to Stephanie Handel and Trudy Post-Sprunk, who so generously donated their time to review my manuscript, providing me with insight and valuable suggestions. Acknowledgment and appreciation is extended to the many talented colleagues who graciously took the time to try the activities with their clients, and who offered helpful feedback. I am also grateful to Nancy Boyd-Webb and William Steel for their pioneering work with bereaved children and for their words of support.

Thanks to Fern Rubinstein, for her editorial guidance, and to my dear friend Sally Schoellkopf, for proofreading the manuscript. Thanks also to the staff at Hignell Printing, for their helpful input.

A special thanks to my family and friends for their continued support and encouragement. In particular, I am deeply indebted to my husband, Steven, for his unconditional love, and for making sacrifices that gave me the time and support needed to write this book. Finally, I am forever grateful to my precious daughter, Jaime, who brings joy to my life each and every day.

Liana Lowenstein
May 2006

Introduction

When children enter therapy because they have experienced the death of a family member or close friend, they are at a very vulnerable time in their lives. They are often anxious about the therapeutic process and reluctant to talk directly about the death. Activities that are creative and play-based can engage children and help them to express their thoughts and feelings. The purpose of this book is to provide mental health professionals who work with bereaved children with creative interventions to engage, assess, and treat them. A range of innovative activities are presented, including therapeutic games, art, puppets, role-plays, and stories. Studies have demonstrated the effectiveness of these play-based interventions for children (Utay & Lampe, 1995; Burroughs, Wagner, & Johnson, 1997; McCarthy, 1998; Johnson et al., 1998). Most of the activities in this book have been developed for children ages 7 through 12, but many can be modified for both younger and older children.

Practitioners using this book should have clinical training and a sound knowledge base in: child development, attachment theory, psychopathology, childhood trauma, childhood bereavement, and child therapy. A list of suggested readings and professional training associations is provided at the end of the book for those who wish to broaden their knowledge. The activities presented here can be integrated into any theoretical orientation that uses a directive child therapy approach. Thus, practitioners from a wide range of theoretical orientations will find many activities to incorporate into their therapy sessions.

The first section of this book, which contains guidelines for practitioners, lays the foundation for effective grief counseling with children. Section Two presents a theoretical overview of childhood bereavement and it incorporates some of the latest literature on children's bereavement. Additional reading on the topic can be found in the *References and Suggested Readings* section. The third section provides material for use with the child's caregivers. It includes a letter to give caregivers in the first session, informing them about the therapeutic process, and a social history questionnaire to be used as part of the clinical assessment. A handout on bereaved children is also included, which will help caregivers better understand and respond to their child. The remaining sections offer assessment and treatment tools and interventions. Special sections have been included to assist children in dealing with specific kinds of loss, namely cancer, suicide, and homicide. In addition to individual therapy activities, there are also sections with interventions for children's bereavement groups and family sessions. An overview for practitioners is presented at the beginning of each section, to provide clinical guidelines for how to use the interventions. The appendix includes: a sample letter for the practitioner to give to the child upon termination from therapy; a treatment plan; a handout on bereaved children to give school personnel; and resources for children, caregivers, and professionals.

The interventions in this book have been specially designed to capture and sustain children's interest and motivation in therapy, and to help bereaved children approach their grief within the context of a safe therapeutic environment. Practitioners can make an enormous difference in the lives of bereaved children by providing them with a positive and engaging therapeutic experience.

Contents

Activities at a Glance

ACTIVITY	GOAL	AGES	MODALITY
Feel Better Bag	Implement adaptive coping techniques	7-12	I,G
About Me	Begin to articulate thoughts and feelings	7-12	I,G
Getting To Know Each Other	Establish therapeutic rapport	7-12	I
Feeling Faces Cut 'N Paste	Identify range of feelings regarding the death	7-10	I,G
Feelings Tic-Tac-Toe	Identify a range of different feelings	7-12	I,F
My Special Person's Death	Verbalize feelings & reactions regarding the death	7-12	I,G
How I Think, Feel, and Behave	Identify stresses, symptoms, coping strategies	7-12	I
Butterflies in My Stomach	Identify stresses, supports, problem-solving	7-12	I,G
People in My World	Identify feelings toward self, family, community	7-12	I
How My Body Reacted	Identify sensory triggers and intrusive thoughts	7-14	I
Life's Ups & Downs	Identify significant life experiences	8-16	I
Ali and Her Mixed-Up Feeling Jar	Identify and express feelings regarding the death	6-10	I,G
My Story	Tell the story with decreased levels of anxiety	8-12	I
Shock and Denial	Identify feelings of shock and denial	7-12	I,G
Feeling Scared and Worried	Identify fears and worries	7-10	I,G
My Body Doesn't Feel Good	Identify psychosomatic complaints	7-10	I,G
Feeling Sad	Identify and express feelings of sadness	7-12	I,G
Feeling Lonely	Implement adaptive coping techniques	7-12	I,G
Feeling Angry	Express anger through appropriate outlets	7-12	I,G
Feeling Like It's My Fault	Eliminate self-blame statements for the death	7-12	I,G
Getting Rid of Guilt	Eliminate self-blame statements for the death	7-12	I,G
Getting Into Trouble	Identify feelings, reduce oppositional behavior	7-12	I,G
Making My Special Person Proud	Verbalize positive thoughts about self	7-14	I,G
Why Bad Things Happen	Verbalize positive thoughts about the world	7-14	I,G,F
Heads or Tails Feelings Game	Identify and express feelings regarding the death	7-12	I
Life and Death	Verbalize understanding of life and death	4-10	I,G
About Death Puzzle	Verbalize understanding of death	7-10	I,G
What Causes Death	Verbalize understanding of causes of death	7-12	I,G
What Happens After Death	Verbalize understanding of death	7-12	I,G
The Funeral	Verbalize understanding of death, Identify feelings	6-10	I,G
Game About Life & Death	Verbalize understanding of death	7-12	I,G,F
My Special Person	Preserve memories of the deceased	7-12	I,G,F
What I Liked and Didn't Like	Identify ambivalent feelings toward the deceased	7-12	I,G,F
Memory Tape	Preserve memories of the deceased	7+	I,F
A Penny For Your Thoughts	Preserve memories of the deceased	7-12	I,G,F
Keepsakes	Preserve memories of the deceased	7+	I,G,F
Wish My Special Person Was Alive	Increase positive thinking	7-10	I,G
Saying Goodbye	Communicate unfinished business to the deceased	7-12	I
Feeling Good About Myself	Identify positive traits about self	7-12	I,G
Coping With Bad Dreams	Implement adaptive coping techniques	7-10	I,G
Coping With Scary Thoughts	Implement adaptive coping techniques	7-12	I
Good Can Come From This	Make meaning of the loss	9-14	I,G,F
I Deserve To Be Happy	Verbalize positive thoughts about future	7-12	I,G
Coping With Grief Attacks	Implement adaptive coping techniques	7+	I,G,F
Feel Good Messages	Implement adaptive coping techniques	7-12	I,G
Coping With Grief Game	Implement adaptive coping techniques	7-12	I,G
What I Learned	Review therapeutic gains	7-12	I
Giving a Helping Hand	Articulate helpful message to other children	7-12	I,G
Special Person Died From Cancer	Verbalize understanding of cancer, express feelings	7-12	I,G,F
Special Person Died By Suicide	Verbalize understanding of suicide, express feelings	7-12	I,G,F
Special Person Was Murdered	Verbalize understanding of homicide, express feelings	7-12	I,G,F
Balloon Bounce	Establish Group Rapport	7-12	G
Group Card Game	Express thoughts and feelings regarding death	7-12	G
Scavenger Hunt	Express thoughts and feelings regarding death	7-12	G,F
Pizza Party	Review therapeutic gains, provide positive termination	7-12	G
Family Gift	Assess family dynamics	All	F
Family Card Game	Increase communication in family	7+	F
Family Changes	Verbalize and adapt to changes in family	7-12	F
Memory Book	Preserve memories of the deceased	4+	F
Candle-Lighting Ceremony	Commemorate the deceased, preserve memories	4+	F, G
Honor & Remember Our Loved One	Commemorate the deceased	All	F
Postcards	Increase communication in family	7-12	F
Nightly Snuggle	Parents provide child with nurturance	7-12	F
Our Family Can Shine	Identify feelings of hope, return to activities of daily life	7-12	F

Modality: I= Individual Therapy, G= Group Therapy, F=Family Therapy

Section 1

GUIDELINES FOR PRACTITIONERS

Have a Strong Theoretical Foundation

Practitioners should be well grounded in their theoretical orientation before using any activities or techniques in therapy sessions with children. Interventions should not be used indiscriminately or in a manner that ignores clinical theory. The activities in this book can be integrated into any theoretical orientation that uses a directive child therapy approach.

Be Well-Informed in Child Language Acquisition

Many of the activities in this book depend on language as the primary means of communication, and require the child to have language mastery. The practitioner therefore must be well-informed in child language acquisition, and only use the activities in this book with children who have the capacity to comprehend the activities and, where needed, verbalize their thoughts and feelings.

Use Activities That Are Appropriate for Each Client

There are a variety of activities to choose from in this book. The child's developmental capacities should be considered to ensure that the selected activity is age-appropriate. (The *Activities at a Glance* has been included to guide the practitioner in this regard.) The child's interests should also be considered so the activity appeals to him or her and sustains his or her motivation. Select activities to fit the child's treatment goals. Pacing is also important. Consider the child's level of engagement in therapy and degree of defensiveness before implementing activities that are more emotionally intense, or that require the child to take greater emotional risk.

Involve Primary Caregivers and the Family in Therapy

Whenever possible, the child's primary caregivers should be involved in the treatment. The caregiver may be a parent, stepparent, foster parent, grandparent, childcare worker, or some other adult responsible for the care of the child. When primary caregivers are included in treatment, their children generally experience greater improvement. By facilitating optimal communication between children and their caregivers about the death, caregivers can continue to help children after therapy has ended. Lack of follow-through with therapy, or premature termination of the child's therapy, is less likely if the caregivers are part of the process.

Bereaved children need physical and emotional comfort, reassurance, and consistent routine. Educating caregivers about how to understand and respond to the needs of bereaved children is also an important treatment goal. Thus, sessions with caregivers to facilitate effective parenting should be a part of the treatment process.

If the deceased person is a family member, then the child's caregivers and siblings will be dealing with their own grief issues. Efforts should be made to involve the whole family in therapy. Although the interventions in this book have been developed for individual sessions with the child, many of the activities can be adapted for family therapy. There is also a special section in this book that presents interventions for use in family sessions.

Be a Support to the Child's Teacher

Bereaved children often struggle at school. For example, they may have difficulty concentrating on schoolwork, or present behavioral difficulties during class. With the client's consent, the practitioner can be a helpful resource to the child's teacher and other school personnel. By providing the child's school with information on bereaved children, teachers can then respond with greater sensitivity to the needs of their students. An information sheet for school personnel is included in the Appendix and can be copied for this purpose.

Develop a Therapeutic Rapport

Regardless of the activity being used, the therapist-client relationship is central to the client's realization of treatment goals. Since rapport that develops between therapist and child forms the foundation for therapeutic success, the practitioner must create an atmosphere of safety in which the child is made to feel accepted, understood, and respected.

Conduct a Thorough Assessment and Develop a Treatment Plan

The clinical assessment is a critical component of the intervention process, as it is the basis for effective treatment planning. A thorough and comprehensive assessment should examine specific bereavement issues, loss history, behavioral and emotional changes and concerns, as well as other presenting problems. An assessment should always be completed prior to beginning treatment. Therefore, the assessment interventions in Section Four should be completed prior to using any of the treatment interventions.

If the child and family are in crisis, the assessment should be completed in a timely fashion, and crisis support should be offered in the interim. Crisis work offered during the assessment phase should focus on strengthening supports and coping skills.

Selected assessment activities from this book can be combined with additional assessment information, family interviews, collateral reports, and diagnostic measures to evaluate the child and his or her family, and to formulate a treatment plan. The treatment plan should set realistic, measurable goals, and be revised as needed with caregivers, the treatment team, and (if appropriate) the child. A Sample *Treatment Plan* is included in the Appendix.

Once the assessment is completed, a meeting with the caregivers should take place to provide feedback on the assessment, consider treatment recommendations and contract for service.

Understand the Difference between Clarification and Correction

During the assessment phase, the goal is to understand and clarify the child's perceptions about self, others, and the world. For example, in an assessment activity, if the child says, "My mom's death was my fault," an appropriate clarification response from the practitioner would be, "Tell me why you think it is your fault." During the treatment phase, the goal shifts to doing corrective work, or challenging the child's cognitive distortions.

Give Each Client a Scrapbook

It is recommended that the child be given a scrapbook in the first session in which to place activities completed during sessions. The scrapbook has several benefits: it allows the child to see the progression of sessions; it provides immediate tangible reinforcement of each therapeutic success; and it gives the child a lasting record to have once therapy is terminated.

All therapeutic activities completed by the child during sessions should be placed in the scrapbook, and it should be kept in a locked place in the practitioner's office. It can be given to the child in his or her last session, with a discussion regarding who, if anyone, should see it, and where in the child's home it should be kept to ensure its privacy. (A complete copy of the scrapbook must be made for the practitioner's file prior to giving it to the child.) For further information about the use of therapeutic scrapbooks, refer to the article, *The Resolution Scrapbook as an Aid in the Treatment of Traumatized Children* published in the Journal of Child Welfare, July 1995 (this article can also be found on the author's web page: www.lianalowenstein.com

Give Each Client a Feel Better Bag

Encouraging self-care and teaching healthy coping strategies is important to do with clients. It is particularly crucial for bereaved children dealing with the death of a family member, since their caregivers may be consumed with their own grief and may not be able to meet the child's emotional needs. It is also important to teach coping skills at the beginning of the intervention process when working with children with traumatic bereavement, so they can master these skills prior to facing anxiety provoking material during treatment. The *Feel Better Bag* is used as a tool to facilitate self-care. This bag is given to the child in the first session to take home, and in each subsequent session the child is provided with a self-care item to add to the bag. Ideas for the *Feel Better Bag* are incorporated throughout this book. In order to encourage the child to use the *Feel Better Bag*, it is recommended that the child's caregiver coach the child on its use at home. In addition, the practitioner should ask the child at the beginning of each session whether s/he used the *Feel Better Bag*, and whether it was helpful.

Maintain a Consistent Structure to Sessions

Each session should adhere to a similar structure, so the child knows what to expect. It can be helpful to begin each session with a check-in ritual to assess current functioning and facilitate self-expression. For example, the client can be asked to rate his or her week on a scale of one to ten (one being terrible and ten being perfect), or draw a feeling face to show how s/he feels. The client can also be asked if s/he used a strategy from his or her *Feel Better Bag* and how it helped him or her to cope better. A quick engagement activity can then be played, such as *Feelings Tic-Tac-Toe* (see Section Four).

Next, the child can complete the activity or activities planned for the session. (The practitioner should be prepared to divert from the planned activity if needed.) The child can then choose an activity to do, such as a board game, craft, or playing with toys in the room. Some children will need a more energetic activity at the end of the session to appropriately channel excess adrenalin caused by anxiety. As mentioned above, all completed activities should be placed in the child's scrapbook, and the child should be provided with something to take home to add to his or her *Feel Better Bag*.

Be Well-Prepared in Advance of Sessions

Before using any assessment or treatment exercise, the practitioner should first review the activity and gather any necessary materials. If the practitioner lacks confidence, then practicing and rehearsing the activity with a colleague before the session may be helpful. However, no matter how well prepared the practitioner is for the session, the unforeseen can happen. Flexibility in meeting children's emotional needs over the sessions is therefore essential.

Introduce, Process, and Bring Closure to Each Activity

When implementing an activity, first consider how it will be introduced to the child. The therapist's enthusiasm, creativity, and overall style will be key factors in determining if the child will become interested and engaged in the activity. All activities should be carefully processed and used as a point of departure for further discussion. The practitioner can encourage the child to elaborate by asking open-ended questions such as, "Tell me more about that," or by inquiring about a particular detail of the child's work. As the child moves to a more engaged and ready state, deeper issues can be skillfully explored and processed. When the activity has been completed and sufficiently processed, the therapist provides positive feedback to the child on his or her completed work and brings closure to the activity.

Set Appropriate Limits

Bereaved children often "act out" as they feel overwhelmed by their grief, and may lack the capacity to handle their strong emotions. It is necessary to provide the child with limits and structure. The nature and intensity of the limits will depend on the child's existing capacity for self-control, as well as his or her responsiveness and ability to handle such limits. Ideas to manage such behaviors can be found in the author's book, *More Creative Interventions for Troubled Children and Youth*.

Recognize the Impact of Grief on Affect and Behavior

Children's emotional presentation in therapy may be related to where they are in their grieving process. For instance, if they are in the initial stages of grief, i.e. shock and disbelief, they may present as emotionally numb or detached. Or if they are in the anger stage, they may be highly susceptible to aggressive outbursts or fits of rage. If they have been traumatized, they may be in a constant state of anxious-arousal (which is often misdiagnosed as ADHD). Recognizing the impact of grief and trauma will help the practitioner better respond to the child's needs.

Be Sensitive to Cultural and Religious Customs and Beliefs

Clients will have specific religious beliefs about death, and will practice certain grieving rituals based on their culture and religion. It is important to honor these beliefs and be accepting of diversity. Practitioners should never impose their beliefs onto clients. Information should be gathered about the client's religious background and grieving rituals during the assessment.

Model Open and Direct Communication about Death

Many people find it difficult to talk openly and directly about death, and so they may use indirect terms, such as "gone" or "passed away." In order for practitioners to model open and honest communication, direct and accurate terms about death should be used when working with bereaved clients.

Provide a Positive Termination Experience

The termination phase of treatment must be handled with sensitivity, particularly with bereaved children who may experience the end of therapy as another loss. During this phase of the intervention process, the child may experience feelings of sadness, anger, rejection, and abandonment. Termination can also be a wonderfully positive experience as the child's therapeutic progress and achievements are highlighted and celebrated.

A graduation ceremony can be planned for the last session with the child, to help create a positive, celebratory atmosphere for this important phase of intervention. If appropriate, caregivers can be invited to the ceremony. The practitioner can write a letter to present to the child at the graduation ceremony. This letter will review goals achieved in therapy, validate the child's efforts and accomplishments, reinforce healthy thoughts, and provide a positive message for the child's future (see Appendix for a sample letter). The practitioner can also ask other people who are significant to the child to write letters for presentation to the child at the ceremony. The letters can be placed at the end of the child's scrapbook.

Obtain Professional and Personal Support

Working with bereaved children can be professionally and emotionally challenging. It is, therefore, important to obtain supervision from a clinician who is knowledgeable in the area of treating bereaved children. It is also important to make use of support from colleagues and friends, and engage in regular self-care rituals.

Section 2

Bereaved Children: A Brief Theoretical Overview

Clinicians using this book should be well-trained in issues specific to bereaved children. Below is a brief summary on various aspects of children and grief. Suggestions for additional reading can be found in the *References and Suggested Readings* section in the Appendix.

Key Definitions

Grief describes the intense emotions one experiences following a loss.

Bereavement refers to the state or fact of having lost a loved one by death.

Mourning refers to the external expression of grief, or the rituals associated with bereavement.

Disenfranchised grief refers to grief that is not socially acknowledged or supported. It is often related to a stigmatized kind of death, such as suicide, drug overdose, or AIDS related death. It can also refer to a relationship loss that is not socially validated, such as grieving the death of a murderer.

Trauma results when an individual is exposed to an overwhelming event leading to helplessness and a diminished capacity to cope and master the feelings aroused by the event.

Traumatic bereavement refers to when children perceive the death as horrifying or terrifying, and both grief and trauma issues are present. A child can experience traumatic bereavement even if it was not a violent death. Children who develop traumatic bereavement get "stuck" on the traumatic aspects of the death and cannot proceed through the normal bereavement process. They may experience symptoms of a traumatic stress reaction: anxiety, nervousness, a heightened startle response, nightmares and sleep disturbances, and intrusive memories of the death. For children with traumatic bereavement, trauma symptoms must be treated before children can move forward with the grieving process (Cohen et al. 2001).

Children's Bereavement Responses

Regardless of their age, all children grieve. The chart on the next page summarizes children's bereavement responses at different developmental stages. However, as Webb emphasizes, "Development is an individual process that proceeds generally as outlined, but as with all matters human, individual variations occur frequently" (1993, p. 5). Moreover, the chart is a general summary and cannot include all possible reactions.

Children's Bereavement Responses at Different Developmental Stages
(Adapted from McKissock, 2004)

Age	Concept of death	Grief response	Signs of distress	Suggestions
Birth-2	-Death as separation and/or abandonment	-Sense rather than understand person is gone	-Difficulty toileting, sleeping -Clinginess -Temper tantrums -Crying	- Simple, honest explanation of death with familiar examples - Physical comfort -Consistent routine
2-4	-Death as abandonment, sleep, temporary, reversible, contagious	-Intense, brief response -Present oriented -React to changes in routine and care -Ask repeated questions -Anxious about basic needs being met	-Regression (lapses in toilet training, returning to security blanket or old toys) -Anxiety at bedtime -Fear abandonment -Seek physical contact -Irritable, tantrums	- Simple, honest explanation of death with frequent repetition - Physical comfort -Consistent routine -Reassurance that death not contagious, will be taken care of -Allow some regression
4-7	-Death still seen as temporary, reversible	-Feel responsible for death due to magical thinking, i.e. "I was mad at her and wished she'd die. I made it happen." -Repetitive questioning: How? Why? -May act as though nothing happened -Feel distressed and confused	-Overt signs of grief such as sadness, anger -Feelings of abandonment and rejection -Changes in eating and sleeping -Nightmares -Violent play -Behavioral problems -Attempt to take on role of person who died	-Simple, honest explanation of death, avoid euphemisms, e.g. sleep, gone away, lost -Check to see if understand explanation -Expect repeated questions - Opportunities to express feelings, learn coping strategies - Reassurance that they are not responsible for the death
7-11	-May still see death as reversible, but beginning to see it as final -Death as punishment for bad behavior, bad thoughts -Fear of bodily harm and mutilation	-May feel angry or responsible for the death -Desire for details about the death, specific questioning -Concerned with how others are responding and whether they are reacting the right way -Starting to have ability to mourn and understand mourning	-Overt signs of grief such as sadness, anger -Physical complaints -Overactive to avoid thinking about death -Feel ashamed, different from other children -Problems in school, withdraw from friends, acting out -Concern with body -Suicidal thoughts (desire to join the deceased) -Role confusion	-Open, honest explanation of death -Answer questions -Opportunities to express range of feelings -Learn skills to cope with anger, provide physical outlets -Reassurance not responsible for the death
12-18	-Death as inevitable, universal, irreversible -Abstract thinking -Truly conceptualize death	-Depression, denial, repression -More apt to talk to people outside the family -May feel embarrassed -Place peer needs ahead of family -Traditional mourning	-Depression, anger, non-compliance -Difficulty concentrating -Withdrawal from family -Engaging in high-risk behaviors (sexual promiscuity, drug and alcohol use)	-Direct, open dialogue about the death -Encourage verbalization -Listen -Consistent limits balanced with more freedom and choices -Do not attempt to take grief away

ᵵ Factors

According to Worden (1996); there are a number of factors that render a bereaved child vulnerable to increased difficulties:

• Sudden deaths, suicides, homicides
• Death of a mother for girls before, or in, early adolescence
• Death of father for pre-teen and adolescent boys
• Stigma associated with, or media focus on, suicide or homicide
• Conflictual relationship with deceased person prior to death
• Lack of reality, unable to spend time with deceased person after death
• Inadequate preparation for funeral
• Pre-existing psychological difficulties
• Psychologically vulnerable parent, i.e. dependent on child, drugs/alcohol
• Lack of family and community support
• Unstable environment, i.e. disruptions of routine, inappropriate discipline
• Poor family coping, i.e. lack of open communication, poor problem-solving
• Immediate dating by surviving parent
• Remarriage of surviving parent if child's relationship with stepparent is negative

The more risk factors present, the greater difficulty the child will have coping with the death. Knowing what risk factors the child is dealing with will enable the practitioner to intervene more effectively. When there are a number of risk factors, longer term intervention with the child and family by a multidisciplinary team is generally the treatment of choice.

Grief-Focused Treatment Goals

Although an individually tailored treatment plan must be developed for each client, there are a number of grief-focused goals that should be addressed in the treatment of bereaved children (Worden, 1996, Cohen, et al. 2001):

1. Accept the reality and permanence of the death
2. Experience the painful emotions of the death, such as sadness, anger, confusion, guilt
3. Recognize and resolve ambivalent feelings toward the deceased
4. Adjust to changes in everyday life
5. Identify and preserve positive memories of the deceased
6. Redefine the relationship with the deceased as one of memory
7. Develop new relationships and deepen existing relationships
8. Make meaning of the loss
9. Foster enhanced problem-solving and conflict resolution

The activities in this book have been developed with the above goals in mind in order to facilitate the client's grieving process.

The Issue of Closure

A common issue pertaining to the treatment of bereaved clients is closure. Closure is defined as "a conclusion or an end." But closure is an unrealistic goal, as bereaved individuals do not conclude or end their grieving process. A more realistic goal for bereaved children is for the intense pain of the loss to "no longer be psychologically dominant in one's daily life" (Fink, 2002, p. 7). The child is then able to have a healthy capacity for trust, to have a more hopeful outlook of the future, make memories of the deceased, reengage with the community, and function productively. Although no longer dominant, the pain of the loss is not over. One continues to grieve the death, although with lowered levels of intensity. Various events, such as the anniversary of the death date, family celebrations, etc. are likely to intensify painful feelings for a period of time (Fink, 2002, p. 7). For this reason, preparing children for future painful feelings, or "grief attacks," is an important treatment goal.

Section 3

Meeting with Caregivers

It is recommended that the primary caregivers be interviewed prior to meeting the child. The focus of this initial session is on establishing a positive rapport with each caregiver, explaining the therapy process, completing administrative forms, and learning about the child and family. Some caregivers may be reluctant to meet with the child's therapist. This may be due to their fear that they will be negatively judged. The practitioner must make every effort to engage the primary caregivers. One strategy is for the practitioner to communicate to the caregiver (in a caring tone) that the child's therapy will be seriously hindered without their participation.

Letter: The letter (see following sample) can be given to caregivers in the initial session. It covers information about the therapist's role and the therapeutic process.

Questionnaire: Detailed information should be obtained from all primary caregivers as part of the assessment process. The questionnaire collects the following information:

• The child's current living arrangements
• The child's developmental history
• The child's relationship with the deceased prior to the death
• Circumstances surrounding the death
• Feelings and reactions about the loss
• Family information
• Parent history

The information on the questionnaire should be collected via a face-to-face interview with the caregivers. This facilitates rapport-building, and allows the practitioner to elicit more detailed information than would otherwise be obtained if the caregiver were to complete it on his or her own. The practitioner needs to be cognizant of the fact that gathering detailed information regarding the circumstances of the death can be a sensitive issue as it evokes emotionally laden memories for the grieving caregiver. For this reason, the practitioner must be especially careful about establishing rapport with these clients before delving into details related to the death.

Handout: The handout, *How Bereaved Children Think, Feel, and Behave And What Adults Can Do To Help,* provides caregivers with information on children and grief, and with tips on how to help grieving children. The hope is that this information will better equip caregivers to respond to the special needs of their children. It is suggested to review and process the handout with caregivers, rather than simply giving it to them to read on their own.

Letter to Caregiver

Dear Caregiver,

I have prepared this letter to provide you with some information about my role, the therapeutic process, and what to expect from therapy. It is my hope that this information will help us work better together so we can be a supportive team for your child. My role is to provide a safe therapeutic environment in which your child can openly express his or her thoughts and feelings. Since children typically have difficulty talking about their issues, I use play-based activities, such as therapeutic games and art, to make it easier for them to express themselves.

I will begin by completing an assessment on your child. The information that you provide to me about your child will be an important part of this assessment. I may also request to meet with your family as part of the assessment, as this can help me develop a better understanding of your child's needs. Once I have completed my assessment, I will provide you with feedback and make recommendations.

It is not the goal of therapy to "fix" children or to take away the pain of children's normal grief emotions. The goal of grief therapy is to help children mourn the death in a healthy way. This involves helping children face painful feelings a little at a time, and teaching them skills to cope with these painful feelings. Each child is unique and requires a treatment plan geared especially to his or her needs. We will work together to develop realistic treatment goals.

As therapy progresses, you may notice some changes in your child's behaviors and symptoms. For example, your child may experience an increase in the following: nightmares, fears, aggression, or difficulties concentrating. This is normal as your child begins to confront his or her grief. If this becomes a concern, we can meet to discuss how to best support you and your child during this time.

You may wonder what to tell your child about the death. Children need simple but honest information about what happened. If you are unsure what to say to your child, I can help you figure out what to say. You may also be unsure what to tell your child about coming to therapy. It can be helpful to say, "You are going to see someone whose job it is to help children with their feelings when someone close to them has died. You will be doing some talking and some playing together. You can tell this person anything."

It is important that you bring your child to therapy as scheduled and on time. Children feel more secure and do better in therapy when they have consistent appointments. Please do not talk about concerns regarding your child to me in front of your child. This usually makes children feel uncomfortable. If you would like to discuss a concern, please call me prior to the session. Please ensure your child cannot hear the phone conversation. Many children find it uncomfortable when their caregivers ask them details about their sessions. It is helpful to ask your child a more general question, such as, "How was your session today?" The child can then decide what he or she feels like sharing. I certainly understand your concern and interest in your child's therapy, and we will meet regularly to discuss your child's progress. Please note that I am obligated by law to report any safety concerns to legal authorities.

Your reactions and behaviors will influence your child's reactions and behaviors. If you are having difficulty coping, it is important that you seek help so that you can get the support that you need and be a stronger support for your child. It is also important to know that your child will do better if you are involved in the therapy. We will discuss this further so we can come up with a plan that makes sense for both you and your child. I encourage you to call me if you have any concerns that cannot wait until our next scheduled appointment.
Sincerely,

_____

(Signature of Therapist)

Questionnaire for Primary Caregivers

Child's Name: _____ Date of Birth: _____ Address:_____
Mother's Name: _____ Date of Birth: _____ Occupation: _____
Father's Name: _____ Date of Birth: _____ Occupation: _____
Home Phone #: _____ Mother's Work/Cell #: _____ Father's Work/Cell #: _____
Child's School: _____ Teacher: _____ Grade: ____ Phone #: _____
Who has custody of child? _____ (If divorced, provide copy of custody order for file)

List all those living in child's home:

Name	Relationship	Age/School /Occupation

List other persons closely involved with child but not living in the home:
_____
_____

What are your concerns about your child that made you bring him/her to therapy?
_____
_____
_____

List any complications at birth, delays in development, serious health issues:
_____
_____
_____

List any ongoing health concerns/allergies/medications your child is taking and for what purpose:
_____
_____

Describe any serious life stresses child experienced, other than the death (abuse, traumatic experiences, etc.)
_____
_____
_____
_____

Describe prior assessment/therapy child has received (Name of professional, date of service, diagnosis):
_____
_____

Describe any significant losses child experienced prior to this one, and impact the loss had on the child:
_____
_____

Describe how child was coping prior to the death:
_____
_____

Relationship of the deceased to child: Mother___ Father___ Sibling___ Friend/Relative(specify) _____

What was child's relationship like with the person who died? Conflictual___ Fairly close___ Very close___

Date of the death and child's age at time of the death_____

What was the cause of death? _____
Did the child witness the death? Yes___ No___ Please elaborate: _____
_____

Did the child have an opportunity to say goodbye to the person before the death? If yes, please elaborate:
_____
_____
_____

What was the child told about the death, and how did the child react to being told?
_____
_____
_____

Did child view body, attend funeral/burial? (Describe child's involvement in funeral, child's reactions):
_____
_____
_____

Describe child's expression of grief (words, tears, anger, withdrawal, acting out, regression, numbness):
_____
_____
_____

Please describe any concerns about your child listed below:
Difficulty sleeping/ frequent nightmares: _____
Bedwetting or soiling: _____
Unusually clingy or immature behavior: _____
Excessive fears: _____
Change in eating habits: _____
Little sense of joy/happiness: _____
Physical complaints (stomachaches, headaches): _____
Frequent tantrums: _____
Aggressive with others: _____
Hurts self on purpose/talks of wanting to die: _____
Hurts animals on purpose: _____
Sets fires: _____
Lies/steals: _____
School difficulties: _____
Difficulties relating to peers: _____
Inappropriate sexual behavior: _____
Other: _____

Is there any other important information you would like to share about your child?
_____
_____
_____

Would you give permission for your child to receive food or candy during sessions? Yes___ No___

Family Information

Describe the family response (How others in the family are coping with the death, whether family talks openly about the death, participates in mourning rituals together):

_____
_____
_____
_____
_____
_____

Describe child's relationship with parents/caregivers and siblings:

_____
_____

Who is a support to the child and how is this support expressed?

_____
_____

Describe any family conflict related to the death/not related to the death:

_____
_____
_____

Describe family religious practices, mourning rituals, cultural beliefs about the death, life after death:

_____
_____
_____
_____

Has the child/family visited the grave since the death? (If yes, describe child's reactions):

_____
_____
_____
_____

Who generally disciplines the child and how is the child disciplined?

_____
_____

Please describe any other concerns about your family (health, mental illness, alcohol/drug abuse, physical/sexual/emotional abuse, marital difficulties, etc.):

_____
_____
_____
_____
_____
_____
_____
_____

On a scale of 1-10 (1= not coping well and 10 = coping well) how do you think you (parent) are coping with the death? Please elaborate:

_____
_____

Mother's Background:

Where were you raised and by whom? Describe past/current relationship with your parents:

_____
_____

List brothers and sisters, their ages, whereabouts, current relationship you have:

_____
_____

Who were you closest to when you were a child? Describe your relationship with that person:

_____
_____

Describe any of the following you/your family experienced during childhood and how it affected you (physical/ sexual abuse, neglect, abandonment, spousal abuse, divorce, other trauma):

_____
_____
_____
_____

How were you disciplined and by whom?

_____
_____

Describe the happiest time/experience you recall from your childhood:

_____
_____

Describe the saddest time/experience you recall from your childhood:

_____
_____

Describe if you or any relatives have ever had any of the following:
Serious illness: _____
Depression/Bipolar Disorder: _____
Anxiety Disorder: _____
Obsessive-Compulsive Disorder: _____
Learning Disability/ADHD: _____
Eating Disorder: _____
Alcoholism/Drug Abuse: _____
Criminal Conviction: _____

Please add any other information about your background that you feel is important:

_____
_____
_____
_____
_____
_____
_____
_____
_____

Father's Background:

Where were you raised and by whom? Describe past/current relationship with your parents:
_____
_____

List brothers and sisters, their ages, whereabouts, current relationship you have:
_____
_____

Who were you closest to when you were a child? Describe your relationship with that person:
_____
_____

Describe any of the following you/your family experienced during childhood and how it affected you (physical/sexual abuse, neglect, abandonment, spousal abuse, divorce, other trauma):
_____
_____
_____
_____

How were you disciplined and by whom?
_____
_____

Describe the happiest time/experience you recall from your childhood:
_____
_____

Describe the saddest time/experience you recall from your childhood:
_____
_____

Describe if you or any relatives have ever had any of the following:
Serious illness: _____
Depression/Bipolar Disorder: _____
Anxiety Disorder: _____
Obsessive-Compulsive Disorder: _____
Learning Disability/ADHD: _____
Eating Disorder: _____
Alcoholism/Drug Abuse: _____
Criminal Conviction: _____
Please add any other information about your background that you feel is important:
_____
_____
_____
_____
_____
_____
_____

Background of Other Primary Caregiver (i.e., Stepparent, Foster Parent):

Where were you raised and by whom? Describe past/current relationship with your parents:

_____

_____

List brothers and sisters, their ages, whereabouts, current relationship you have:

_____

_____

Who were you closest to when you were a child? Describe your relationship with that person:

_____

_____

Describe any of the following you/your family experienced during childhood and how it affected you (physical/sexual abuse, neglect, abandonment, spousal abuse, divorce, other trauma):

_____

_____

How were you disciplined and by whom?

_____

_____

Describe the happiest time/experience you recall from your childhood:

_____

Describe the saddest time/experience you recall from your childhood:

_____

_____

Describe if you or any relatives have ever had any of the following:
Serious illness: _____
Depression/Bipolar Disorder: _____
Anxiety Disorder: _____
Obsessive-Compulsive Disorder: _____
Learning Disability/ADHD: _____
Eating Disorder: _____
Alcoholism/Drug Abuse: _____
Criminal Conviction: _____

Please add any other information about your background that you feel is important:

_____

_____

_____

_____

_____

_____

How Bereaved Children Think, Feel, and Behave, And What Adults Can Do To Help

Children experience many different thoughts and feelings when they are grieving. The following brief summary of children's experiences of grief suggests how caregivers can best respond to the needs of bereaved children.

Shock and Denial

Shock is one of the first feelings children experience when a family member or close friend has died. They may <u>think</u> the person is not really dead, or is coming back. They may <u>feel</u> little or no emotion. They may <u>behave</u> as if everything is fine. Adults sometimes have difficulty understanding how children can be laughing and playing when someone they love has just died. However, this stage of shock and denial allows children to block their emotional pain, so they can face their grief at a slower pace, when they are ready. While it is important to allow children this initial period of denial, it is <u>not helpful</u> to hide the truth about the death or to reinforce their denial by saying something like, "Daddy will be home soon." It is <u>helpful</u> to talk to children about the death honestly and directly, and in a way they will understand. The book, *Talking About Death* by Earl Grollman is a useful guide. Saying things like, "Be strong," or "Big boys don't cry" is <u>not helpful</u> as this encourages children to hide their emotions. It is <u>helpful</u> to accept children's apparent lack of feelings as a normal response, while at the same time giving them permission to openly express their emotions. For example, it is helpful to say, "You may feel nothing at all right now, or you may feel very upset and feel like crying--whatever you feel is okay, and you can talk to me about anything." Children will more readily confront the reality of the death and express their emotions when they feel comfortable and safe.

Disorganization and Panic

Bereaved children often experience a heightened sense of disorganization or panic. They may <u>think</u>, "Who will take care of me now?" or "Will I or someone else I love die too?" They may <u>feel</u> scared, insecure, confused, or overwhelmed. They may <u>behave</u> by appearing irritable, hyperactive, or unfocused. They may complain of frequent headaches or stomachaches, or have trouble sleeping or eating. They may become regressed or clingy in an effort to get comfort, or they may act older than their years as a way of trying to feel in control. It is <u>not helpful</u> to reprimand the child. It is <u>helpful</u> to reassure the child by saying things like, "Even though I feel sad, I am going to be okay and I am here to take care of you," or "Even though the doctors could not make your sister better, most people live a long and healthy life," or "You and I both went to the doctor for a check-up and we are healthy." Providing children with comfort and reassurance will support them through this difficult time.

Explosive Emotions

Sometimes bereaved children exhibit explosive emotions, such as rage, blame, terror, and jealousy. They may <u>think</u> their life is out of control. They may <u>feel</u> overwhelmed. They may <u>behave</u> by acting out. It is important to allow children to express their strong emotions, so they do not turn their anger inward. It is <u>not helpful</u> to discourage the expression of feelings, or to be punitive. Rather, it is <u>helpful</u> to encourage the healthy expression of emotions, while setting appropriate limits. A three-step process can be used:

1. Label the child's feelings, i.e. "You are angry because dad is not here to play baseball with you."
2. Set a limit, i.e. "It's okay to be angry but it's not okay to let out your anger by punching your sister."
3. Provide an appropriate alternative, i.e. "You can let out your anger by punching a pillow."

It is <u>helpful</u> to understand the needs that underlie children's acting-out behavior. For example, children may be communicating a need to be comforted, reassured, or empowered. Talking to children about their feelings and validating their anger will help them express their emotions, rather than repress their grief.

Guilt

Many children blame themselves when someone they care about dies. Young children, in particular, may blame themselves because they believe that by thinking about something, they can make it happen. This is called magical thinking. For example, in anger a child may say, "I hate you, I wish you were dead!" and then when that person dies, they believe their angry thoughts caused the death. Children may also believe their misbehavior caused the death. They may <u>think</u> "It's all my fault." They may <u>feel</u> like they are bad or worthless. They may <u>behave</u> by directly or indirectly seeking punishment, or by acting good in order to bring the person back to life. In addition to blaming themselves for the person's death, children may also blame themselves for the grief of those around them. For example, if they see a parent crying, they may believe it is their fault. Some children may feel guilty because they are relieved their loved one is dead, particularly if the person who died was ill for a long time or the child's relationship with the person who died was conflictual. It is <u>not helpful</u> to avoid discussing the child's guilt, as this is likely to push the feelings underground. It is also <u>not helpful</u> to simply say, "It's not your fault" as this is telling the child how to feel, rather than exploring the child's feelings. It is <u>helpful</u> to provide opportunities for the child to talk openly about his or her feelings, and to help the child understand that his or her thoughts or behavior did not cause the death. For example, it is <u>helpful</u> to open the dialogue by saying, "Sometimes kids think the death is all their fault. There are many reasons why kids feel guilty. Do you ever feel like you did something to cause the death?" *After* the child has expressed his or her feelings, it is important to reassure the child by saying something like, "It is very sad that mom died, but nothing you said or did caused her to die." For children who cannot articulate their feelings of guilt, it is <u>helpful</u> for adults to express warmth and acceptance both verbally and non-verbally. If a child is made to feel loved and valued, this will help alleviate feelings of guilt and shame.

Sadness

As children begin to acknowledge the reality and finality of the loss, their sadness begins to surface. They may <u>think</u>, "Mom is gone and is never coming back." They may <u>feel</u> depressed, empty, alone, or hopeless. They may <u>behave</u> by crying, or by being sullen and withdrawn. Often these feelings surface long after the death, when adults fail to make the connection to the death that occurred months or even years earlier. But it is important to understand that this is a time when children are particularly vulnerable and are in need of support. It is <u>not helpful</u> to ignore or discount the child's feelings, or give the message that he or she should "be over it by now." It is <u>helpful</u> to encourage the child to openly express feelings of sadness. Children who have difficulty verbalizing their feelings may feel more comfortable drawing about their sadness.

Acceptance

People, both children and adults, do not "get over" grief, but feelings do lessen in intensity over time. At some point in the grief process, children come to accept the reality of the loss. It is at this point that children think, "Daddy is gone, I miss him, but I'm going to be okay." They feel a renewed sense of energy, hope, and confidence. They behave by being more joyful and by becoming re-involved in activities. It is not helpful to rush the child along or to have expectations about how and when a child should grieve. It is helpful to be patient, and allow children to grieve in their own way and in their own time. It is also helpful to recognize that children revisit grief at various points throughout their lives. There will be times when they have "grief attacks" when strong feelings of loss come rushing back. "Grief attacks" can often be anticipated, as they are often triggered by special days such as the anniversary of the person's death, holidays, birthdays, graduations, etc. It is helpful to talk about potential "grief attacks" ahead of time and ensure the child feels supported. For example, caregivers can say to a child, "Tomorrow is your birthday and you may have some mixed-up feelings. You may feel happy and excited, but you may also feel sad or angry because mom isn't here to celebrate this special day. Whatever you are feeling is normal and okay. Your mom would be very proud of you because you are such a terrific kid!"

Summary

Children do grieve, but how they grieve is different than adults. Whereas adults can more readily verbalize their feelings, children typically express their feelings through their behavior. Therefore, adults need to pay particular attention to how children behave, in order to gauge their level of distress. Moreover, children will grieve in a healthier way if they feel safe and supported, and if those around them are grieving in healthy ways. Caregivers have a major impact on children and play an important role in easing children through the difficult task of grieving. There are many ways to help bereaved children. By acknowledging what children are thinking, validating what they are feeling, and responding sensitively to how they are behaving, caregivers can help children deal with their grief.

Below are some suggested books for caregivers wishing to learn more about how to help grieving children:

Talking About Death: A Dialogue Between Parent and Child by Earl Grollman

Helping Children Grieve & Grow by D. O'Toole

Continuing Bonds: New Understandings of Grief by D. Klass, P. Silverman, & S. Nickman

But I Didn't Say Goodbye by B. Rubel (Helping children cope with suicide)

What Parents Need To Know by B. Steele

Section 4

Interventions to Engage & Assess Bereaved Children

Each child presents his or her own unique set of emotional, cognitive, and behavioral issues. Many children have difficulty verbalizing their concerns because they are reluctant to self-disclose and are anxious about the therapeutic process. Activities that are creative and play-based can engage otherwise resistant children, and can help them to express their thoughts and feelings. This section provides a number of interventions to engage and assess bereaved children. While these activities provide useful strategies to engage children, it is the therapist's use of self that is most powerful in engaging children. The therapist's warmth, consistency, and unconditional acceptance of the child are the key ingredients to put children at ease and help develop a therapeutic rapport.

Rationale for Conducting a Thorough Assessment

The ultimate purpose of assessing children is to offer them treatment that is as effective and efficient as possible. A comprehensive clinical assessment should be conducted for the following reasons:

- Determines whether the child needs treatment, and if so, what needs to be treated
- Enables the practitioner to tailor treatment to the child's needs
- Provides direction on best treatment modality, i.e. Individual, group, family
- Enables the practitioner to provide accurate feedback to caregivers on the child's needs
- It is cost effective, since it shortens the length of treatment as it enables the therapist to hone in on exactly what needs to be treated

Areas to Assess

The clinical assessment is a critical component of the intervention process, as it forms the foundation for effective treatment planning. A thorough assessment generally requires between three and six 60-minute sessions. The following areas should be examined as part of the assessment process (Lieberman, et al., 2003; Webb, 1993):

- The child's emotional, social, and cognitive functioning before and after the death
- The child's relationship with the deceased
- The circumstances of the death, i.e. anticipated/sudden, degree of pain, presence of violence, element of stigma
- The child's contact with the deceased, i.e. present at death, viewed dead body, attended funeral/burial, visited grave/mausoleum
- The child's grief reactions
- The child's expression of "goodbye"
- Traumatic reminders of the death
- Disruptions of daily routines
- The child's relationships with family, peers, and community
- Cultural and family beliefs and traditions regarding death and mourning
- The family's grief reactions and ability to communicate openly about the death

- The family's strengths and vulnerabilities in caring for the child
- Other major stresses in the child's life

It is important to determine whether the child is experiencing traumatic bereavement or is merely struggling with adaptation to the loss. This is an important distinction, because children with traumatic bereavement require trauma-specific treatment before their bereavement issues can be addressed (Lieberman, et al., 2003).

Sources of information for the assessment include: (a) Information from primary caregivers (see *Questionnaire for Primary Caregivers* in Section Three); (b) Information from collateral sources; (c) Individual sessions with the child; and (d) Sessions with the family (see Section Eleven).

The Engagement and Assessment Process

This section includes engagement and assessment tools and techniques. The engagement activities precede the assessment interventions, because a therapeutic rapport must be established prior to beginning the assessment.

Many bereaved children are reluctant to trust. For this reason, the practitioner must be especially careful about establishing rapport and building a trusting relationship with these clients before delving into details related to the death. There are a number of ways the practitioner can encourage trust and promote openness with clients. A warm, accepting, and attentive therapeutic manner is important.

Some children may be resistant to exploring their bereavement issues. The practitioner can help the child overcome avoidance by openly discussing their fears and reluctance to talk about distressing material at the beginning of the assessment process. The *Welcome Letter* covers this to some extent, but the practitioner can expand on this issue.

During the assessment of bereaved children, control of the pace is critical. It is important to be cognizant of non-verbal signs of discomfort if a child is reluctant to speak up. Some children may be very compliant even when they are in distress. If the child does need to take a break from an assessment activity or stop talking about a particularly distressing issue, it can be helpful to switch to an activity that fosters coping, so the child does not feel helpless. It is important to make a statement about coming back to the activity or issue at some later time when the child feels ready. This conveys the message that avoidance of distressing events is not a healthy long-term coping strategy.

During the assessment, maintaining a calm and accepting manner will help the child feel supported. Normalizing, validating, and reflecting the child's feelings will reassure the child and communicate understanding.

Once the child has completed each assessment activity, it is helpful to discuss and explore the child's responses to glean additional information. Asking open-ended questions is a particularly useful strategy for eliciting richer information from the child.

After the assessment is completed, the practitioner analyzes and interprets the data that has been collected. The accuracy of the conclusions gathered from the assessment depends largely on the skills of the assessor. No one source of information provides a definitive evaluation of children's functioning. Instead, practitioners must obtain different perspectives on children and then integrate information across multiple sources. The practitioner must integrate and compare the information gleaned from the assessment with: (a) knowledge of normal age-appropriate developmental issues; (b) the acquired details about the child's current issues as well as past histories; and

(c) the information regarding the child gathered from other sources, i.e. parent reports, teacher reports, psychological/psychiatric assessments, etc. The information gathered from the assessment is used to make recommendations for intervention,and, where appropriate, suggestions for further assessment.

Engagement Interventions

The Welcome Letter: The initial session with the child should focus on rapport building. The child can be provided with his or her scrapbook, and the *Welcome Letter* can be placed on the first page. The *Welcome Letter* can be read to the child to engage him or her, normalize feelings, clarify the therapist's role and duty to report safety concerns and explain basic rules and the format of sessions. The letter can be modified for group counseling, i.e. the purpose of the group, the role of the group leaders, and group rules.

The Feel Better Bag: The child can be given the *Feel Better Bag* in the first session. The purpose of the *Feel Better Bag* is to encourage self-care and to teach healthy coping strategies. This is particularly important for children who have limited social support. It is helpful to teach the child some coping strategies early in the intervention process, so he or she can use these strategies if s/he becomes anxious during a session or at home. The child can be provided with something to take home to add to the *Feel Better Bag* at the end of each session. In order to encourage the child to use the *Feel Better Bag*, it is recommended that the child's caregiver coach the child on its use at home. In addition, the practitioner should ask the child at the beginning of each session whether s/he used the *Feel Better Bag*, and whether it was helpful.

About Me, Getting to Know Each Other: These are appropriate interventions to use in initial sessions as they engage the child and help to develop rapport. Playing the *Getting to Know Each Other Potato Chip Game* helps break through the child's resistance and facilitates open communication.

Assessment Interventions

Feeling Faces Cut N' Paste: This activity normalizes feelings associated with grief, and teaches feeling words to enhance the child's vocabulary. It helps the child express thoughts and feelings regarding the death, which is an important therapeutic goal. Modify for older children by having them draw feeling faces, and then writing about their feelings.

Feelings Tic-Tac-Toe: Most children are familiar with *Tic-Tac-Toe* and will enjoy this version of the game. As the child talks about his or her feelings, the practitioner can reflect the child's feelings, ask the child to elaborate, and praise the child for his or her openness. When it is the practitioner's turn to share, the practitioner should tailor his or her own responses in a way that would be therapeutically beneficial to the child. *Feelings Tic-Tac-Toe* can also be played at the beginning of each session to reengage the child and quickly assess any pressing issues.

My Special Person's Death: The Dice Game: This activity ascertains the child's knowledge about the death, initial grief reactions, the child's perceptions of how family members are grieving, concerns regarding the death, and available supports. The game format makes the child feel more comfortable and will help the child begin talking about the death.

How I Think, Feel, And Behave: This activity provides rich assessment information regarding the child's grief reactions, as well as their intensity. Several statements on the worksheet pertain specifically to trauma symptoms, and therefore assess whether the child is suffering from traumatic bereavement. This activity allows children to identify their clinical issues without having to verbalize them directly, and so it is particularly useful with children who have difficulty talking about their problems. The practitioner should wait until the child has finished placing the self-adhesive dots on the worksheet before asking the child about his or her responses, so as to not affect the processing phase.

Butterflies in My Stomach: As part of the assessment process, it is important to explore the child's general presenting problems, as well as problem-solving skills, coping abilities, and available supports. This intervention is particularly useful with children who have a multitude of presenting problems, as it enables children to communicate to the therapist which problems are most pressing and need priority in treatment.

People in My World: This activity assesses family and community relationships and available support networks. It also evaluates feelings such as sadness, anger, fear, and self-blame. The child should include self and significant family and community members on the worksheet (both positive and negative relationships) so that these relationships can be assessed. The stickers are a useful tool to engage children in the activity.

How My Body Reacted: This activity should only be used with children experiencing traumatic bereavement. It assesses sensory assault and other trauma responses such as avoidant behavior and intrusive thoughts. Since the activity may trigger flashbacks or anxiety, it can be helpful to teach or review a previously learned relaxation strategy prior to beginning the activity, so the child can use the strategy to self-soothe if needed.

My Life's Ups & Downs: This activity assesses significant events in the child's life, and normalizes that everyone has both positive and negative life experiences. In processing negative events in the child's life, the practitioner can highlight the child's resilience and coping abilities. Once the child has completed writing the events, the practitioner guides the child to discuss in more detail each memory and his or her feelings associated with each memory. It is important for the practitioner to emphasize that everyone experiences "ups and downs" in life.

Letter to Child

Welcome _____,
(Child's Name)

You are here today because someone you cared about died. Kids who are dealing with the death of a special person usually have lots of feelings, thoughts, and reactions. This is called grief. It may take a while for you to sort out these feelings and start to feel better again. This is a place where you can come and talk about your feelings. You may feel worried, nervous, or scared about coming here today, but hopefully you'll feel better as we get to know each other.

My job is to listen to you and to help you through this difficult time. My job is also to help keep you safe, so if someone is hurting you, it is really important that you tell me so I can talk to the adults whose job it is to help and protect children.

In order for us to feel safe and okay in here, it is important that we both follow some rules: We don't hurt anybody or break anything on purpose, and we don't take anything out of the room without permission.

Each time you come here, we will do some talking and some playing. Many children do not want to talk about upsetting things like when someone dies, but getting your feelings out can help you feel better. Since it can be hard to talk about death and painful feelings, we will use drawing activities and games to make it easier for you to share your feelings.

All your hard work will be kept in this scrapbook and it will be locked in a safe place here in the office. On your last day of coming here, you can either take your scrapbook home, or you can leave it in the office where it will be kept in a safe, private place.

If you'd like, you can take some time now to decorate the cover of your scrapbook.

I look forward to talking and playing with you!
From,

_____
(Therapist's Name)

Feel Better Bag
(Supplies: Gift bag)

You have probably been feeling sad and upset since your special person died, but there are things you can do to help yourself feel better. Today, you are going to get a special bag. It is called a *Feel Better Bag*. Each time you come here, you will get something to put in your *Feel Better Bag* that can help you feel better.

You can take your *Feel Better Bag* home today, and you can use it when you are feeling upset. Talk with your therapist about where to keep your *Feel Better Bag*, so you can use it when you need to.

Although your therapist will give you ideas of things to add to your *Feel Better Bag*, you can always add your own ideas. Remember that this special bag belongs to you, and you can use it in whatever way helps you most!

Turn the page to find out the first thing you get to put in your *Feel Better Bag*.

Something for Your Feel Better Bag:
A Hug
(Supplies: Hershey's Chocolate Hug)

Dealing with the death of a special person can be difficult but it can help to get a hug from someone you care about, or to give yourself a hug. Put this Chocolate Hug in your *Feel Better Bag* as a reminder to hug yourself or ask for a hug when you need one.

After you have eaten your chocolate hug, keep the wrapper in your *Feel Better Bag* as a reminder that hugs can help you feel better.

About Me

Let's begin by getting to know you. Fill in the sentences below:

My name is _____. I am ____ years old. I am here because someone special to me died. His/her name is _____
and he/she was important to me because_____. Here are some other important things about me:

People I live with:

My favorite things to do:

Things I am especially good at:

Draw a picture or glue a photo of yourself in the space below:

Something for Your Feel Better Bag: Feel Better List

There are activities you enjoy doing, people you feel close to, and things you are good at. There are many things that can make you feel better. Make a "Feel Better" list (a list of people, places, and things that make you feel better). Put your "Feel Better" list in your *Feel Better Bag*. Look at it when you feel sad as a reminder that there are people, places, and things that make you feel better.

My Feel Better List

People who make me feel better:

Places that make me feel better:

Things I do that make me feel better:

Getting To Know Each Other: The Potato Chip Game
(Supplies: Small bag of potato chips)

Getting to know each other better will help you feel more comfortable here, and make it easier for you to share your thoughts and feelings. So let's play a game to get to know each other better. It's called *The Potato Chip Game*. To play, take turns asking each other a question from the list below (or you can make up your own questions). If a player answers the question, he or she gets a potato chip. If the player does not answer the question, the other player gets the potato chip. Continue the game until you have asked each other all the questions. Remember, you get a potato chip for every question you answer!

1) What's something you like doing?
Me: _____
My Therapist: _____

2) What's your favorite color?
Me: _____
My Therapist: _____

3) What's one of your favorite foods?
Me: _____
My Therapist: _____

4) What's one of your favorite movies?
Me: _____
My Therapist: _____

5) What's something that really bugs you?
Me: _____
My Therapist: _____

6) What's one of the best things you ever did?
Me: _____
My Therapist: _____

Something for Your Feel Better Bag:
My Therapist Cares about Me

The Potato Chip Game helped you get to know your therapist. Write down some things you learned about him or her. Put your list in your *Feel Better Bag*. When you are upset, look at the list and remind yourself that this person cares about you and is there to help.

What I learned about my therapist:

Feeling Faces Cut N' Paste
(Supplies: Scissors, Glue)

Dealing with the death of a special person can bring many feelings. These kinds of feelings are called grief. You probably have many different feelings about the death of your special person. At times, you may have strong feelings and at other times you may feel nothing at all. The *Feeling Faces Cut 'N Paste* activity will help you talk about your feelings. Look at the feeling faces below, and cut out the ones you feel about your special person's death. Cut along the dotted lines. Glue them on the next page, then write underneath each feeling about why you feel that way.

SHOCKED
Don't expect something to happen

SCARED
Afraid when something bad happens

NERVOUS
Thinking something bad is going to happen

NUMB
No feelings at all

CONFUSED
Don't know what something means

RELIEVED
No longer worried about something

HAPPY
Glad because something good happened

GUILTY
Feeling bad for something you think you did wrong

JEALOUS
Upset when you don't have something someone else has

SAD
Unhappy or upset

PROUD
Feeling good about something you did well

LOVED
Feeling cared for

ANGRY
Upset when you don't like what happened

LONELY
Feeling all alone

(Add any other feelings you have about your special person's death)

My Feelings about My Special Person's Death

Glue Feeling
Face Here

I feel this way about my
special person's death because:

_____
_____
_____
_____

Glue Feeling
Face Here

I feel this way about my
special person's death because:

_____
_____
_____
_____

Glue Feeling
Face Here

I feel this way about my
special person's death because:

_____
_____
_____
_____

Glue Feeling
Face Here

I feel this way about my
special person's death because:

_____
_____
_____
_____

Glue Feeling
Face Here

I feel this way about my
special person's death because:

_____
_____
_____
_____

Glue Feeling
Face Here

I feel this way about my
special person's death because:

_____
_____
_____
_____

Glue Feeling
Face Here

I feel this way about my
special person's death because:

_____
_____
_____
_____

Glue Feeling
Face Here

I feel this way about my
special person's death because:

_____
_____
_____
_____

Glue Feeling
Face Here

I feel this way about my
special person's death because:

_____
_____
_____
_____

Glue Feeling
Face Here

I feel this way about my
special person's death because:

_____
_____
_____
_____

Glue Feeling
Face Here

I feel this way about my
special person's death because:

_____
_____
_____
_____

Glue Feeling
Face Here

I feel this way about my
special person's death because:

_____
_____
_____
_____

The Feelings Tic-Tac-Toe Game
(Supplies: Two different kinds of small wrapped candy, 4 of each kind)

It can be hard to talk about feelings but sometimes playing a game can make it easier. To play this special version of *Tic-Tac-Toe* use candy instead of X's and O's. Players take turns placing their candy on one of the nine squares on the game board in an attempt to get either an uninterrupted horizontal, vertical, or diagonal line of three. As the candy pieces are placed on the game board, players describe a time they experienced that particular feeling. Players can eat one candy each time they win a round.

Happy	**Angry**	**Nervous**
Scared	**Loved**	**Guilty**
Jealous	**Sad**	**Relieved**

Something for Your Feel Better Bag:
(Supplies: Two different kinds of small wrapped candy, 4 of each kind)

Add the *Feelings Tic-Tac-Toe Game* Board to your *Feel Better Bag*, along with some candy. Play the game with an adult helper. Playing the game with the adults who care about you is a good way to express yourself and let them know how you are feeling.

Happy	**Angry**	**Nervous**
Scared	**Loved**	**Guilty**
Jealous	**Sad**	**Relieved**

Special Person's Death: The Dice Game
(Supplies: Dice, bag filled with small prizes)

The *Dice Game* will help you share your thoughts and feelings about your special person's death. To play the game, roll the dice, and if you roll an even number (2, 4, 6) answer a question below in order from 1 to 7. If you roll an odd number (1, 3, 5) you get a small prize! Play the game until all the questions below have been answered.

(1) This is who told me my special person died, and what I remember them saying:

(2) This is what I did and felt right after I found out my special person died:

(3) This is how others in my family reacted to my special person's death:

(4) This is what I know about when, where, and how my special person died:

(5) These are two changes in my life since my special person died:

(6) These are my questions and worries I have about my special person's death:

(7) These are the people I can talk to when I feel upset:

Something for Your Feel Better Bag: Tummy Breathing
(Supplies: Small toy)

Helping your body learn to relax is a good way to help yourself feel better. One way to help your body relax is to do *Tummy Breathing*. Lie on the floor, and place a small toy on your tummy. Breathe deeply in and out. Make the toy on your tummy rise during inhaling. Slowly count backward from 5 while breathing in through the nose, and then slowly breathe out through your mouth while again counting backward from 5. As you are slowly breathing in and out, make sure the toy on your tummy rises up each time you breathe in and goes down each time you breathe out. Put the toy in your *Feel Better Bag* as a reminder to practice *Tummy Breathing*. If you practice *Tummy Breathing* at least four times every night before you go to bed, you will learn it so you can use it when you need to help your body relax.

How I Think, Feel, and Behave
(Supplies: ¼" adhesive dots available in label section of office supply stores)

Below are some common ways children think, feel, and behave when a special person dies. Read each statement and stick a dot beside the ones that apply to you. You can put more dots beside the ones you experience a lot.

1. I HAVE MORE WORRIES SINCE MY SPECIAL PERSON DIED_____

2. I HAVE BAD DREAMS_____

3. I TRY NOT TO THINK OR TALK ABOUT THE DEATH_____

4. I FIND IT HARD TO CRY AND FEEL SAD_____

5. I HAVE SCARY THOUGHTS ABOUT THE DEATH_____

6. I SOMETIMES GET STOMACHACHES WHEN I FEEL UPSET_____

7. I'M AFRAID SOMETHING BAD WILL HAPPEN TO ME_____

8. I'M WORRIED ABOUT SOMEONE IN MY FAMILY_____

9. MY FAMILY DOESN'T TALK MUCH ABOUT THE DEATH_____

10. I'M WORRIED ABOUT WHO WILL TAKE CARE OF ME_____

11. I'M WORRIED I CAN NEVER BE HAPPY AGAIN_____

12. SOMETIMES I WISH I WAS DEAD_____

13. I THINK MY SPECIAL PERSON'S DEATH WAS MY FAULT_____

14. I THINK PEOPLE DIE BECAUSE THEY HAVE BEEN BAD_____

15. I DIDN'T GET TO SAY GOODBYE TO THE PERSON BEFORE S/HE DIED_____

16. I THINK THE PERSON WHO DIED WILL COME BACK_____

17. I GET INTO TROUBLE A LOT_____

18. I THINK I'M IN THERAPY BECAUSE I AM BAD_____

19. I'M WORRIED I'M NOT DOING WELL IN SCHOOL_____

20. I GET TEASED BY OTHER KIDS_____

21. SOMEONE IS HURTING ME BUT I'M AFRAID TO TELL_____

22. I'M GLAD I'M GETTING HELP NOW_____

Something for Your Feel Better Bag:
The Spaghetti Technique
(Supplies: Uncooked spaghetti noodle in a zip-lock bag)

You can help your body feel better by learning to relax your muscles. Here's an easy way to learn how to relax your muscles; it's called the *Spaghetti Technique*:

Step 1: Stand up straight and stiff, tighten your body like uncooked spaghetti, hold it for 3 seconds

Step 2: Go limp and wiggle your muscles like cooked spaghetti

Step 3: Make your body go like wet spaghetti until you feel relaxed

Put these instructions in your *Feel Better Bag* as a reminder to practice *the Spaghetti Technique*. If you practice *the Spaghetti Technique* at least four times every night before you go to bed, you will learn it so you can use it when you need to help your body relax.

Butterflies in My Stomach

Everyone has problems and worries, but when someone close to you dies, it can make you feel more worried and scared. This activity will help you talk about your problems and worries. It is called *Butterflies in My Stomach* because when you are worried or nervous about something, your stomach might feel funny or jittery, as if you have butterflies in your stomach. You don't *really* have butterflies in your stomach, it just feels like you do. Write your worries on the paper butterflies on the next page. Write bigger worries on the larger butterflies, smaller worries on the smaller ones. After you write your worries on the butterflies, answer the questions below:

When you are feeling scared or worried, what could you do to help yourself feel better?

Who are some people who can help you with your problems and worries?
What can they do to help?

If your special person who died were here, what advice would they give you about your problems and worries?

Butterfly Outlines

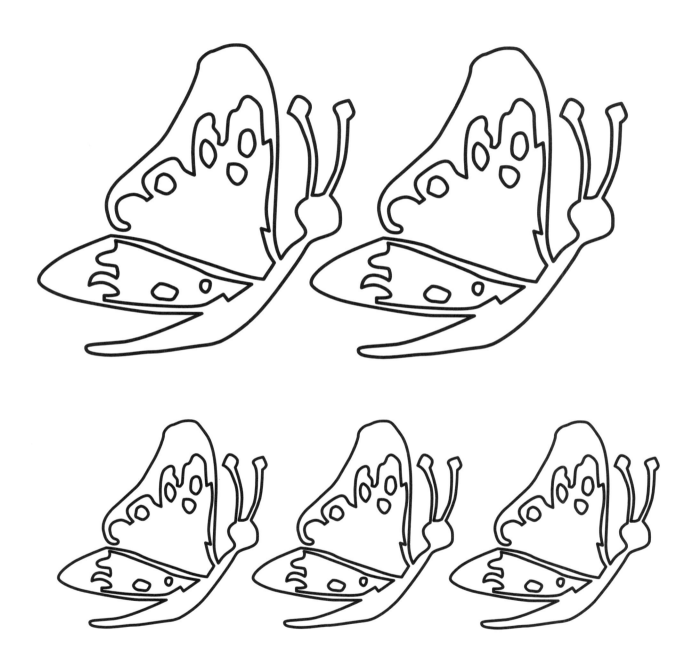

Something for Your Feel Better Bag:
Helping Myself Feel Better

Write down the ideas you listed on the previous page about how to help yourself feel better when you feel scared or worried. Look at this list when you feel scared or worried as a reminder of the things you can do to help yourself feel better.

People in My World
(Supplies: Heart and star stickers, Band-Aids, red and blue ¼" adhesive dots available in office supply stores)

This activity will help you talk about the important people in your world. The first step is to fill in the picture of the world on the next page by writing the names of the people in your world. (Write each name in a different section on the world.) Include people who are important because you feel close with them, as well as people who are important because they have hurt or upset you. Be sure to include yourself, the people you live with, and other people in your family. You may wish to include some of your relatives, baby-sitter, teacher, religious leader, therapist, doctor, best friend, pet, etc. Next, use stickers and symbols for the following feelings:

Put <u>hearts</u> on people in your world who <u>love</u> you. How do they show that they love you?

Put <u>Band-Aids</u> on people in your world who feel <u>sad</u>. Why do they feel sad?

Put <u>red dot stickers</u> on people in your world who feel <u>angry</u>. Why do they feel angry?

Put <u>blue dot stickers</u> on people in your world who feel <u>scared</u>. Why do they feel scared?

Put an <u>"X"</u> on people in your world who are <u>mean or bad</u>. Why are they mean or bad?

Put <u>star stickers</u> on people in your world who <u>help</u> you. What do they do to help you?

People in My World

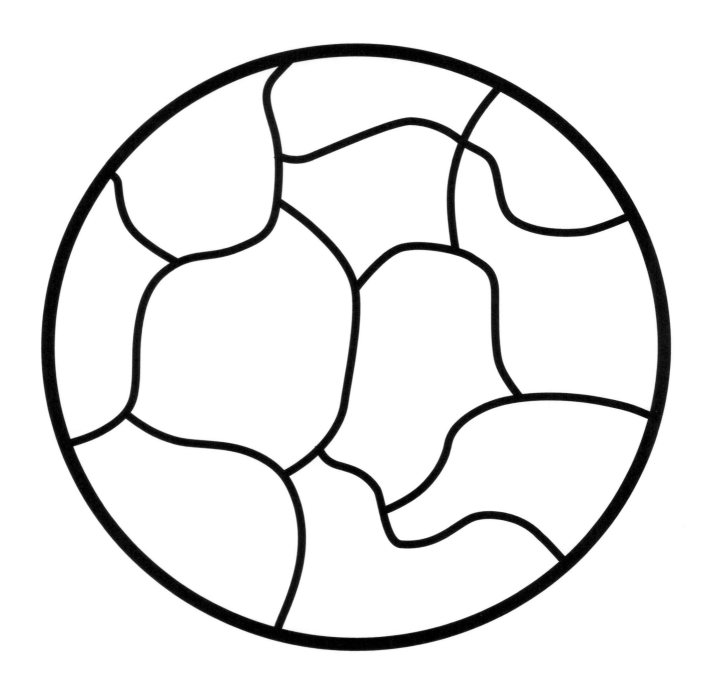

Something for Your Feel Better Bag: People in My World Who Help Me

(Supplies: Star sticker)

Put a star sticker in your *Feel Better Bag* as a reminder that there are people in your world who help you. When you are upset, talk to one of your helpers.

How My Body Reacted

You may have experienced something really horrible, like seeing your special person become very sick, have a bad accident, or get killed. When children experience something like this, their body reacts in different ways. This activity will help us understand how your body reacted. Think back to when the horrible experience happened as you do this activity. Use the paper body outline on the next page to complete the questions below: (If you start to get very upset while doing this activity, tell your therapist and s/he will help you do a relaxation exercise that will help you feel better.)

Describe what happened and where you were when you saw the terrible thing happen: (for example, you saw your special person get hit by a car while playing outside)

Color in your head. What were you thinking right before it happened?

Color in your eyes. What did your <u>eyes see</u> when it happened? How did this make you feel?

Color in your ears. What did your <u>ears hear</u> when it happened? How did this make you feel?

Color in your nose. What did your <u>nose smell</u> when it happened? How did this make you feel?

Color in your mouth. What did your <u>mouth taste</u> when it happened? How did this make you feel?

Color in your hands. What did your <u>hands touch</u> when it happened? How did this make you feel?

What did you want to do when it was happening?

Are there any places you don't like to go because it reminds you of what happened?

How often do you think about what happened: A lot__ Sometimes__ Never__

Think of something you could do that would make you feel better right now:

Body Outline

Something for Your Feel Better Bag:
Shoulder Scrunch

You can help yourself feel better by relaxing your body. One way to relax your body is to do the *Shoulder Scrunch*. To do it, scrunch your shoulders up to your ears, then relax them and move them around until all the tightness and tension is gone. Add these instructions to your *Feel Better Bag*. Do the *Shoulder Scrunch* when you feel tense or upset and it will help you relax.

Life's Ups & Downs
(Supplies: Paper, tape, ruler, 3"x2" self-adhesive labels)

Life is full of ups and downs. We all experience both happy and sad times. Make a time-line of important events in your life, including both the good and bad times. To make a time-line, tape paper together to make one long piece. Use a ruler to draw a line across the middle of the paper. Think about important memories (happy and sad ones) and write each one on a separate adhesive label. Write your age at the time of the memory at the top of each label. Once you have written your memories on the labels, stick them on the time-line beginning with your earliest memory and proceeding in order to more recent memories. Stick your <u>happy</u> memories <u>above</u> the line, and your <u>sad</u> memories <u>below</u> the line. If you are having trouble remembering things, use the following as a guide:

Earliest memory from when I was very young

Happy or sad memories with my family

Happy or sad memories of school

Memories of times I felt excited, scared, mad, guilty, loved

Memories of births, deaths, holidays, vacations, moves

Memories of when I or someone in my family got hurt or very sick

Memories of my achievements or proud moments

Worst day of my life

Best day of my life

Something for Your Feel Better Bag:
Bubble Bath
(Supplies: Bubble Bath)

Taking a bubble bath is a good way to help your body feel calm and relaxed. Add the bubble bath to your *Feel Better Bag* and use it when you need to help your body relax.

Section 5

Interventions to Process Grief Reactions

The activities in this section are focused on processing children's grief reactions. It is normal to experience shock and denial in the early stages of the grieving process. Once the child begins to understand that the person is really gone, grief reactions may include sadness, anger, guilt, fear, and anxiety. Many bereaved children experience physical distress. Some children express their grief by acting out. The games, expressive arts activities, and stories in this section address these common grief reactions.

Interventions

Ali and Her Mixed-Up Feeling Jar: *Ali's Story* can help children explore and discuss their feelings related to the death. Children can identify with Ali, and they can share in her experiences vicariously. Children's sense of isolation may be reduced as they realize that other children, even if they are only fictional characters, have been through similar circumstances. As an alternative to coloring a jar, colored sand can be used to fill a jar.

My Story: This activity should only be used with children experiencing traumatic bereavement. It assists the child in creating a trauma narrative. The practitioner should be trained in the use of trauma narratives before completing this activity with the child. (For further information, refer to *Cognitive Behavioral Therapy for Traumatic Bereavement in Children* published by The National Child Traumatic Stress Network, www.NCTSNet. org.) The activity guides the child to write the details of the death, and read (and re read) the story, until the child no longer experiences intense negative reactions when thinking about the death. The purpose of the intervention is to gradually desensitize the child to thoughts, feelings, and reminders of the traumatic death, in order to alleviate extreme negative emotional reactions and physiological reactivity. The cotton balls are used to help the child communicate levels of distress. The puzzle and treasure at the end serve as positive reinforcements. Expressive arts and play-based techniques can be incorporated into the activity to lower the threat level. For example, the child can add illustrations to their story, use puppets to "tell" their story. After the child has written his or her story, s/he should read it aloud several times, until it can be read with minimal distress. Given the intensity of this activity, it should be done over several sessions. The therapist must pay careful attention to the child's level of distress, and pace the activity according to his or her readiness. Processing of the activity should help the child connect thoughts and feelings. For example, as the child reads a segment of the story, the therapist can ask, "What are you thinking and feeling as you read this part?" Once the child feels comfortable reading the story aloud to the therapist, and it has been processed in sessions, s/he should be prepped to read the story to his or her parent(s) in a separate parent-child session. Prior to the session between the child and parent, the therapist should meet with the parent (without the child) and read the child's story aloud to the parent several times. The parent must demonstrate an ability to tolerate hearing the child's story with minimal distress before conducting the parent-child session. The therapist can prepare the parent for the parent-child session by coaching the parent to make supportive verbalizations to the child. The activity should be prepared by the practitioner in advance of the session as follows: (1) Cut the key into seven puzzle pieces; (2) Fill a small box or treasure chest with the following items: a happy face sticker, a glitter star or star sticker, a Hershey's Chocolate Hug; (3) Write the following message on a small piece of paper and place it in the treasure chest: *Congratulations on earning this treasure! You have worked very hard and you are being rewarded with the following gifts: A happy face for getting your feelings out, a star because you are a super kid, and a chocolate hug because people care about you!* (4) On the outside of the treasure box, write the following: *Use your key to open this treasure.*

Shock and Denial: Since shock and denial are common reactions in the early stages of grieving, this activity normalizes and processes the child's grief reactions.

Feeling Scared and Worried: Many children experience heightened levels of anxiety following the death of someone close. They may worry that they or someone close to them will get hurt, sick or die, or that something else bad will happen. This activity addresses these fears and provides children with appropriate reassurances.

My Body Doesn't Feel Good: Bereaved children may be experiencing physical distress in the form of headaches, stomachaches, tiredness, or difficulties eating or sleeping. It is helpful to normalize these physical reactions, and convey the message that physical symptoms usually dissipate when feelings are more openly expressed.

Feeling Sad: Once children progress to the middle stages of grief and feel the pain of the loss, their sadness will intensify. Some children may not feel they can cry, or they may not have permission to do so. This activity facilitates the expression of sadness, and gives permission for children to grieve freely and openly.

Feeling Lonely: Many grieving children feel lonely and lack family and community support. This activity normalizes feelings of loneliness, expands the child's support network, and strengthens their coping skills.

Feeling Angry: Anger is a real and necessary part of the grieving process. Bereaved children may be angry at themselves if they feel responsible for the death, angry at the person who died for leaving them, angry at others for not saving the person who died, or angry at God for taking their loved one away. They may be internalizing their anger by being depressed or socially withdrawn, or they may be externalizing it by acting out aggressively. Children need to learn healthy ways to express and cope with their anger. This activity facilitates cathartic release, and teaches anger management strategies. In order for these strategies to be most effective, children should be encouraged to practice newly learned skills outside the therapy session. For this reason, the homework exercise is an important component to this activity. Whenever possible, include the caregivers in the session (or at the end of the session) so they can learn and model the anger management techniques and coach children between sessions. Some children will need additional sessions focused on the safe expression of anger before they are ready to learn anger control. If this activity is being used in group, the group members can make their own play dough then have a play dough pounding contest with one another.

Feeling Like It's My Fault, Getting Rid of Guilt, Making My Special Person Proud: Young children are egocentric and often believe that they have caused the events that affect them. As a result, children may believe they caused the person to die. The key to understanding self-blame lies in determining the child's belief system regarding why the death occurred. Children may wonder whether their misbehavior or negative thoughts toward the deceased contributed to the death. Or they may feel guilty for not somehow preventing the death. These interventions provide ways to identify and correct cognitive distortions and to relieve feelings of guilt.

Getting Into Trouble: When children feel overwhelmed by strong negative emotions, they may act out to express their distress, or they may engage in negative attention-seeking behavior in order to elicit care. This activity can help children develop insight into this behavior in order to facilitate positive change.

Wondering Why Bad Things Happen: When children experience a negative or traumatic life event, it may impact their world-view. That is, they are more likely to perceive the self more negatively and the world as more violent and frightening. An important treatment goal to counter this cognitive distortion is to encourage acts that strengthen self-worth and positive thinking about the world. This intervention facilitates this process.

Heads or Tails Feelings Game: Because this game touches on the various issues that were addressed in this section, it helps the child integrate the material. The game format captures the interest of children and helps them verbalize their thoughts and feelings. The active component of the game (the "Tails" list) helps to channel the child's energy into positive outlets.

Ali and Her Mixed-Up Feeling Jar
(Supplies: Assorted colored crayons)

Children dealing with the death of a family member or close friend usually have lots of mixed-up feelings. This activity will help you talk about your feelings. Read *Ali's Story* **then answer the questions below:**

How did Ali feel at first when she was told her mother died?

What did Ali worry about after her mother died?

Why did Ali feel guilty about her mother's death?

How did Ali feel once she talked to her therapist about her feelings?

You may feel the same as Ali about the death, or you may have different feelings. Think of how you feel about your special person's death and make your own *Feeling Jar* **by coloring the jar on the next page. Choose a different colored crayon for each feeling. Use more of one color to show feelings you experience a lot. Complete the chart below to show the colors you chose for each feeling, and to explain your feelings about the death.**

Color	Feeling	Why I feel that way

Feeling Jar

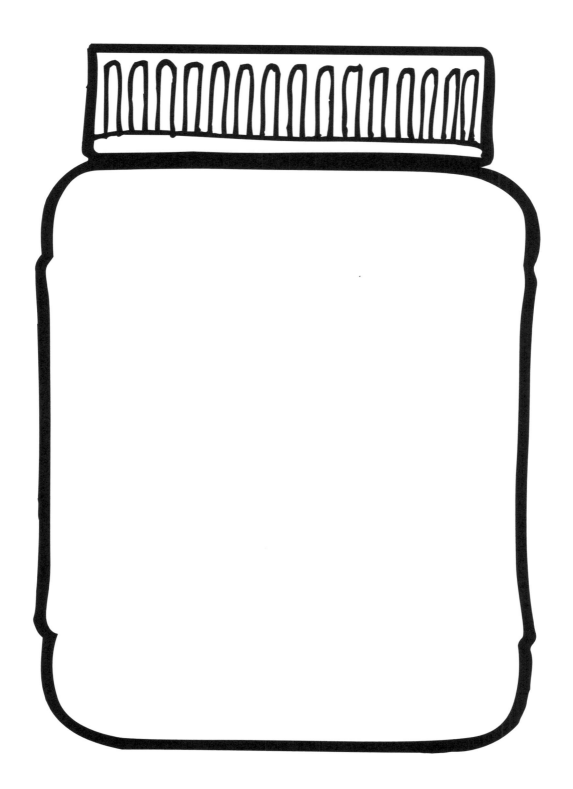

Ali and Her Mixed-Up Feeling Jar

This is a story about a girl named Ali. Her mother died. She has a lot of mixed-up feelings inside her. She remembers the day her dad told her the awful news. He sat her down in the living room and said, "Ali, I have some very bad news to tell you. Your mother died today." At first Ali couldn't believe it. She was **shocked**! She thought it must be a bad dream, and she would wake up and everything would be fine. But it was not a dream. Her mother was dead. Once Ali realized her mother was really dead, she felt so **sad**. But she pretended she was fine because she didn't want to make her dad more upset.

After her mother died, Ali **worried** that her dad would die too. She was **scared** that there would be nobody left to take care of her. Ali wondered if she made her mother die, because once when her mother would not let her have ice cream for dinner she told her mother she hated her and wished she was dead. Ali felt so **guilty** for saying that to her mother. Ali felt **angry** that her mom had died. It was no fair that she had to grow up without a mom. And she felt **jealous** whenever she saw other kids with their moms. Ali often felt **sad** and **lonely**, especially at night when her mom wasn't there to tuck her into bed. Ali got **depressed** because her feelings were so mixed-up: **sad**, **worried**, **scared**, **guilty**, **angry**, **jealous**, **lonely**—all these mixed-up feelings jumbled up inside her. Ali didn't know what to do with all these mixed-up feelings. So she pretended that she had a big jar inside her stomach where she could keep all her mixed-up feelings. It wasn't a real jar of course, but Ali pretended to keep all her mixed-up feelings inside this jar.

Because of all the mixed-up feelings inside her, Ali sometimes did things she never used to, like wetting her bed, and getting into trouble at school. This made her feel like she was **bad**. Often she had scary dreams that would wake her up in the middle of the night. When this happened, she would squeeze her teddy bear really hard until she fell back to sleep.

One night, while Ali's dad was putting her to bed, he said, "Ali, I know it's been hard for you since Mom died. And whatever you are feeling is normal. You won't always feel so upset. Talking about your feelings will help you feel better. You are going to see a therapist whose job is to help kids with their feelings."

The next day, Ali went to see the therapist. At first, Ali felt **nervous** talking to the therapist, but after a while it got easier sharing her feelings. Ali even told the therapist about her pretend jar inside her stomach. As Ali began to talk more and more about her feelings, guess what happened? She began to feel better!

Something for Your Feel Better Bag: Coloring

(Supplies: Crayons)

Add some crayons to your *Feel Better Bag*. Next time you feel upset, let out your feelings by coloring a picture.

My Story
(Supplies: Cotton balls, tape)
(Note to therapist: See section overview for activity preparation and additional supplies)

This activity will help you tell the story about your special person's death. You may not want to think or tell about what happened, but telling the story about your special person's death is a good way to get sad, scared, or angry feelings out, and help yourself feel better. Write your story in as much detail as you can. You can do the writing or you can have your therapist write what you say. You may want to draw pictures to illustrate your story. Each time you complete a part of the story, you get to take a piece of the puzzle. You need to tell all 7 parts of the story to get all 7 pieces of the puzzle. You need all 7 pieces of the puzzle to put the puzzle together to get to the surprise at the end!

As you tell your story, hold cotton balls to show how you feel. If you feel calm and relaxed, hold 1 cotton ball in your hand. If you start to feel sad or scared, hold 2 cotton balls. If you start to feel too sad or scared to continue, hold 3 cotton balls—this will let your therapist know it is time to stop and use a relaxation exercise until you feel ready to continue.

> 1 cotton ball = Relaxed
>
> 2 cotton balls = Sad or scared
>
> 3 cotton balls = Too sad or scared to continue

You should feel calm and relaxed before you begin, and hold onto 1 cotton ball to show that you feel this way. If you do not feel calm before you begin, do a relaxation exercise (your therapist can help you with the relaxation exercise).

When you have finished telling your story, read it out loud from beginning to end. If you start to feel too sad or scared to continue, you can take a break to do a relaxation exercise, and either read it again or come back to it another time.

Your therapist will ask you to read the story again several times in the next sessions. Reading your story out loud several times will help you think about your special person's death without feeling so upset. Eventually, you will be able to think about your special person's death without feeling so sad, scared, or angry, and this will help you feel better! (It is okay to take your time and complete this activity over several sessions.)

My Story

Part 1: About me

Begin your story by <u>introducing yourself</u>: Your name, age, where you live, who you live with, your school and grade, your interests and hobbies.

(Take a piece of the puzzle after you have completed the above section)

Part 2: Before my special person died

Before you write about the day the person died, write about <u>before the death.</u> Tell what your life was like before the person died, how things were in your family, at school, with your friends. Write what you thought and felt about your life before the death.

(Take a piece of the puzzle after you have completed the above section)

Part 3: The day my special person died

Describe in lots of detail what happened <u>the day your special person died</u>. Include <u>who died, how the person died</u>, and exactly what happened. If you don't know exactly what happened, write about what you think happened. (Remember to take more cotton balls if you start to feel more sad or scared as you are telling your story.)

If you saw the person die, write about <u>what you saw, heard, and touched</u>, <u>if you or anyone else got hurt too</u>, if there were any <u>medical or rescue people</u> (police, firefighters, ambulance workers, doctors, nurses) trying to help or save your special person's life.

Tell what you were <u>doing, saying, thinking, and feeling when you saw your special person die</u>. If you were not there when the person died, tell <u>how you found out about the death.</u> Include who told you and what they said to you.

(Take a piece of the puzzle after you have completed the above section)

Part 4: The worst part

Write about the <u>worst part</u> and how you feel as you think about it, like sad, scared, angry, or grossed out. Write how your body feels as you think about this worst part. Write what thoughts come to mind as you think about this worst part.

(Take a piece of the puzzle after you have completed the above section)

Part 5: How my family and I reacted to the death

Describe how you and each person in your family <u>reacted to the death</u>. Tell what you were doing, saying, thinking, and feeling when you found out your special person died.

(Take a piece of the puzzle after you have completed the above section)

Part 6: What it's been like since the death

Describe what it's been like for you and your family <u>since your special person died</u>. Include how you and everyone at home feels, how everyone is dealing with it, what's changed at home, and what you miss most about the person who died.

(Take a piece of the puzzle after you have completed the above section)

Part 7: What I learned

Write what you think you have <u>learned</u> about dealing with the death of someone close, and what <u>advice</u> you would give to other children who are dealing with the death of a family member or close friend.

(Take a piece of the puzzle after you have completed the above section)

Once you have completed all 7 parts of your story, and have 7 puzzle pieces, put the puzzle together and tape it on both sides. Your therapist will then give you special instructions about what to do with the puzzle to get to the surprise!

Key to the Treasure

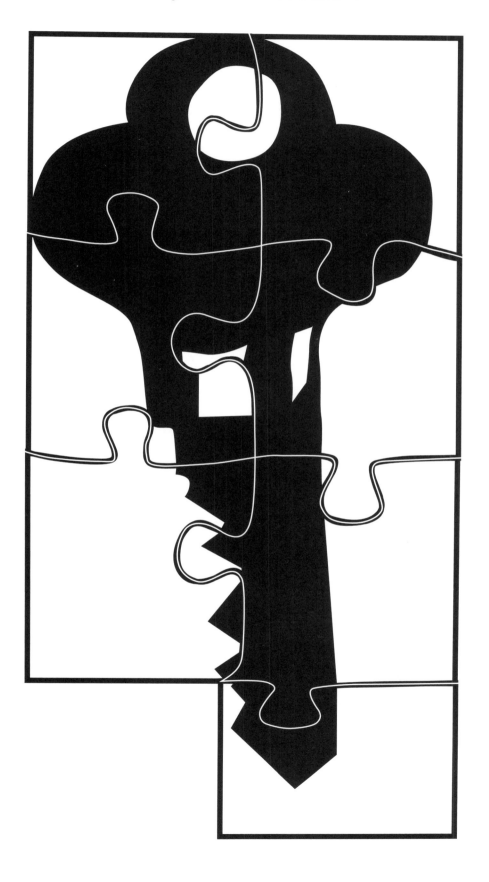

Something for Your Feel Better Bag: Cotton Ball
(Supplies: Cotton ball)

Add a cotton ball to your *Feel Better Bag*. Next time you are feeling sad, scared, or angry, hold the cotton ball. Let it be a reminder that you have gotten yourself through tough times in the past, and you can make it through tough times now.

Shock and Denial

A common reaction after someone dies is to not have any feelings at all. This is called "shock" and it means that you turn off your feelings because you are not ready to deal with the sadness of the person's death. You might be so sad that it is easier to shut off your sad feelings instead of feeling them. You may feel bad because it seems like you should feel sad. But everyone needs to express their feelings when they are ready. Another common reaction to death is denial. You may think that your special person is not really dead because it is too hard to believe they are gone forever. This activity will help you talk about your feelings of shock and denial. Read each statement below and color in the circles to show how you feel. If you totally agree, color in the whole circle. If you agree a bit, color in part of the circle. If you don't agree at all, leave the circle blank.

I try not to think about the person who died: ◯

I don't talk about the person who died: ◯

I find it hard to feel sad when I think about my special person's death: ◯

I tell myself my special person is not really dead and will come back: ◯

I talk about my special person as if he or she is still alive: ◯

I go on with my life as if nothing has changed: ◯

Try not to worry if any of the above statements are true for you. Your reactions are normal and you will face your sadness and accept the reality of your special person's death when you are ready.

Something for Your Feel Better Bag: Four Breathing
(Supplies: 4 stickers)

Taking slow deep breaths is a good way to help your body relax and feel better. Here is an easy way to learn how to take slow deep breaths; it's called the *Four Breathing* technique:

Think of the number **4**. As you are thinking about the number **4**, follow these **4** steps:

Step 1: Breathe in for **4** seconds

Step 2: Breathe out for **4** seconds

Step 3: Wait **4** seconds

Step 4: Repeat this **4** times

Put these instructions and 4 stickers in your *Feel Better Bag* as a reminder to practice *Four Breathing*. Practice *Four Breathing* 4 times this week at bedtime, and take a sticker each time you practice this technique. If you practice this technique you will learn it so you can use it when you need to help your body relax.

Feeling Scared and Worried

You may be feeling more scared and worried since your special person died. You may worry that you or someone you love will get sick and die. It is normal to have these feelings, but it may help to know that most people live for a long, long time. Being sick usually does not mean that someone will die. A doctor can cure most people, or they will get better on their own with rest and medicine. Draw a picture of a time you got sick and tell about what helped you get better:

You may also worry that something bad will happen to you or to someone in your family. But even though bad things sometimes happen, and it's really sad and scary, it's important to realize that there's so much good in the world! Make a list of some good things that have happened to you and to your family:

There may be other things you feel scared and worried about. Talk about your worries with your therapist. Worried feelings usually go away faster if you talk about them and get them out!

Something for Your Feel Better Bag: Call the Girls and Boys Hotline

It is important for you to know that there are always adults available to help children. If you are ever feeling sad or scared, and you do not feel comfortable talking to an adult at home or at school, you can always call the Boys and Girls Hotline. Add the phone number to your *Feel Better Bag*, so you can call it if you have no other adult to talk to about your sad or scared feelings.

Phone number for the Boys and Girls Hotline: 1-800-448-3000

My Body Doesn't Feel Good
(Supplies: Band-Aids)

When you are upset about your special person's death, your body might feel upset too. You may feel more tired. You may have trouble eating or sleeping. You may have headaches or stomachaches or other body pains. This activity will help you talk about how your body is hurting, or reacting to your special person's death. Use the body outline below to put Band-Aids on the parts of your body that feel bad, hurt, or sick. Talk about your hurt with your therapist.

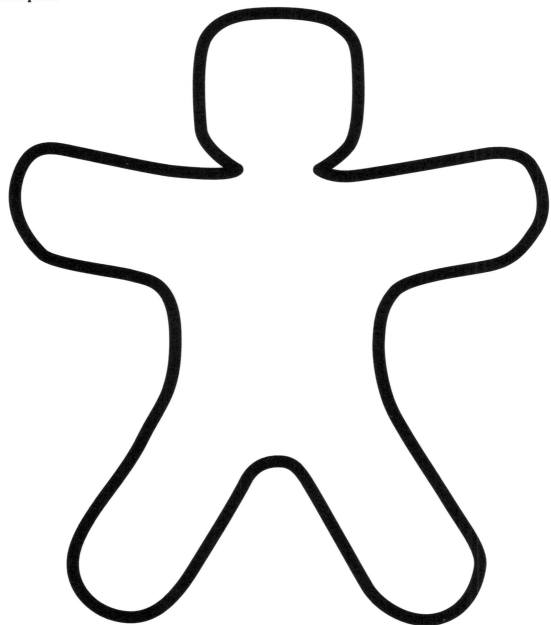

Keeping your feelings all trapped inside can make your body feel sick. Letting your feelings out can help your body feel better. Talking, writing, or drawing about your feelings are all helpful ways to help your body feel better.

Something for Your Feel Better Bag: Exercise

Doing a fun exercise or physical activity is one way to help your body feel better. Look at the list below and circle the ones you would like to do to help your body feel better. Add the list to your *Feel Better Bag*. Next time your body does not feel good, do one of the exercises from the list.

Do jumping jacks

Play music (not too loud) and dance around the room

Skip Rope

Jog on the spot

Lie on the floor and stretch out your muscles

Play basketball with crumpled paper and a garbage can

Put a penny on the tip of your index finger and see how long you can walk around the room without it falling off

Add your own ideas: _____

Feeling Sad

(Supplies: A tissue, tape)

Everyone feels sad at times but when a special person dies, it can make you feel saddest of all. When you feel sad, you may feel like crying. But you may be worried that if you cry, you will make others around you sadder. Or you may think that crying makes you seem weak or look like a baby. But crying is really a very strong and brave thing to do, and it is a good way to let out your hurt. If you don't feel like crying, that's okay too. Not everyone is a crier. This activity will help you talk about your sadness. Copy the questions on the next page onto a tissue, and write your answer to each question onto the tissue. When you are done, tape the tissue in the space below.

Questions about Sad Feelings

When I think about my special person's death, I feel sad because:

When I feel sad I:

When I feel sad I can get help by:

Something for Your Feel Better Bag:
Helping Myself When I Feel Sad
(Supplies: Mini tissue packet, scissors, glue, stickers)

It is important to know that you won't always feel so sad. Feeling sad is a part of grief. Expressing your sadness is a way to help yourself feel better! Below is a list of things that might help you feel better when you are sad. Choose one of the ideas below (or write your own idea), cut it out, and paste it onto a mini tissue packet. Then decorate the tissue packet with the stickers. Add it to your *Feel Better Bag* as a reminder that you can help yourself feel better when you feel sad. If you ever feel like crying, you can use the tissues from your tissue packet.

Things I can do when I feel Sad:

Ask someone for a hug

Cuddle a stuffed animal

Talk about my feelings to an adult

Let out my sadness by coloring a picture

Remind myself I won't always feel so sad

Feeling Lonely
(Supplies: Stickers)

You may be feeling lonely since your special person died. Maybe you feel you have no one to talk to, or to spend time with. But it is important to know that there are things you can do when you are feeling lonely. Put a sticker beside the things below that you can do when you are lonely:

Play with a favorite toy

Listen to music

Do a craft activity like drawing or painting

Play a sport

Write in a journal or diary

Have a silent conversation with your special person who died

Choose one of the above ideas and draw a picture of yourself doing it. Add your picture to your *Feel Better Bag* as a reminder of how to help yourself when you are feeling lonely.

Feeling Angry
(Supplies: Play Dough)

Anger is a common feeling children experience when someone dies. There are many reasons why you may feel angry. You may keep your anger in or you may let your anger out by yelling, hitting, or throwing things. It's important to let your anger out in safe ways. Safe anger means you are not hurting yourself or anyone else when you are expressing your anger. A safe way to let out angry feelings is to pound play dough. (You can make your own play dough by following the recipe on the next page.) Pound the play dough as hard as you can for one minute without stopping. (If you'd like, you and your therapist can have a play dough pounding contest and see who can pound the play dough the hardest and longest!) As you continue to pound the play dough, tell about why you feel angry. (Have your therapist write your angry list in the space below as you pound the play dough.) Pound the play dough hard to show how angry you feel!

I feel angry because:_____
_____
_____

Think about your special person's death and fill in the sentences below:
I am angry because _____
I am angry at _____
It's not fair that _____

Below are some ideas for handling anger in safe ways. Choose one of the ideas from the list and use your play dough to sculpt something that represents the technique. For example, sculpt a Stop Sign for the "Visualize a Stop Sign" technique.

-Visualize a stop sign as a reminder to STOP before I lose control
-Slowly count backward from 20
-Take slow deep breaths until my body feels relaxed
-Talk to an adult
-Other ideas:

Put your play dough sculpture in a zip lock bag. Take it home and add it to your *Feel Better Bag*. It can remind you to use your new technique when you get angry.

Recipe for Play Dough
(Supplies: Bowl, spoon, flour, salt, oil, water, food coloring, garbage bag, tape)

Tip: Tape a garbage bag around the work area to contain the mess

Play Dough

In a medium size bowl, mix together the following:

2 cups of flour

½ cup of salt

2 tablespoons of vegetable oil

Gradually add ½ cup of water and mix together well.
If you need more water, add it a little bit at a time.

Add food coloring to the play dough
(you may want to divide the play dough into several clumps first,
so you can make different colors of play dough).

To keep the play dough soft, place it in a plastic zip-lock bag.

HOMEWORK

(Fill in this section at the end of the session)

Today I learned to handle my anger by: _____

My play dough sculpture will help me remember to: _____

I can practice this technique at home by: _____

My caregiver can help me practice by: _____

· ·

(Fill in this section at home and bring it to your next session)

Situation that made me angry: _____

Safe anger technique used: _____

How this technique helped me: _____

Feeling Like It's My Fault

You may think that you somehow caused your special person to die. Maybe you believe your words caused your special person to die, like if you thought or said, "I hate you! I wish you were dead!" Maybe you think your special person would still be alive if you would have been better behaved. You may think, "I could have done something to stop the death from happening." Or maybe there's another reason why you think you caused your special person to die. Fill in the sentences below to show how you are feeling:

I think my special person's death is my fault because _____

_____

I feel badly that I _____

_____

My special person would still be alive if I would have _____

_____

I wish I could tell my special person that _____

_____

Getting Rid of Guilt
(Supplies: Scissors, glue, markers)

When someone dies, children often feel guilty about it. The word "guilty" means feeling bad for something we think we did wrong. The cartoons on the next pages are about children who feel guilty because of their special person's death. These children received some helpful words of advice from other children to help them get rid of their guilty feelings. Read the cartoons, then answer the questions below. Once you have answered the questions, color in the cartoons, cut them out, and staple the pages together to make a comic book. There are blank cartoons so you can add your own.

What are some reasons why children blame themselves when someone dies?

What words of advice helped the children in the cartoons get rid of their guilt?

Have you ever felt guilty for your special person's death? If yes, why did you feel guilty?

What words of advice can you give yourself to help get rid of your guilt?

Something for Your Feel Better Bag:
Secret Message

Break the code to uncover the secret message below. Then put the message in your *Feel Better Bag*. Whenever guilty feelings creep back in, look at the message to help yourself feel better.

A = 1	N = 14
B = 2	O = 15
C = 3	P = 16
D = 4	Q = 17
E = 5	R = 18
F = 6	S = 19
G = 7	T = 20
H = 8	U = 21
I = 9	V = 22
J = 10	W = 23
K = 11	X = 24
L = 12	Y = 25
M = 13	Z = 26

Example:

<u>3</u> <u>1</u> <u>20</u> = CAT

BREAK THIS CODE

<u>14</u> <u>15</u> <u>20</u> <u>8</u> <u>9</u> <u>14</u> <u>7</u>   <u>9</u>   <u>19</u> <u>1</u> <u>9</u> <u>4</u>   <u>15</u> <u>18</u>   <u>4</u> <u>9</u> <u>4</u>   <u>13</u> <u>1</u> <u>4</u> <u>5</u>
<u>13</u> <u>25</u>   <u>19</u> <u>16</u> <u>5</u> <u>3</u> <u>9</u> <u>1</u> <u>12</u>   <u>16</u> <u>5</u> <u>18</u> <u>19</u> <u>15</u> <u>14</u>   <u>4</u> <u>9</u> <u>5</u>

(See answer on the next page)

Answer to the Secret Code

Nothing I said or did made my special person die

Getting Into Trouble

After someone special dies, children may do things or act in ways they never used to. Sometimes children get into more trouble. This is because they feel so upset, and they find it hard to talk about their upset feelings, so they show their upset feelings by misbehaving. Read *Jason's Story* then answer the questions below.

Questions

1. How do you think Jason feels?

2. Why do you think Jason is getting into more trouble since his dad died?

3. What advice would you give to Jason?

When children get into trouble a lot, they begin to feel that they are bad or no good. But it is important for children to understand that even if their behavior is bad, it does not mean that they are bad. Make a list of some things that are good, special, and lovable about you. Next time you begin to feel that you are bad, remind yourself that you are precious and lovable!

Jason's Story

Hi! My name is Jason. My dad died last year. Everyone in my family is acting really weird now. My mom cries all the time. Sometimes she stays in bed all day and doesn't even get up to make us breakfast. My sister is never around. She hangs out at the mall with her friends and comes home really late, and that makes mom even more upset. My little brother acts like a big baby. He started sucking his thumb and wetting his bed after dad died. And as for me, well, I think I'm going crazy. I do things I never used to do. Like last week, I stole a chocolate bar from the store down the street. I don't know why I did it. I felt bad about it, but then the other day, I stole again—from my best friend. I stuffed one of his computer games into my school bag when he wasn't looking. He caught me when the computer game fell out of my bag as I was leaving his house. He got real mad and told me he didn't want to be my friend anymore. And he told all the kids at school that I'm a thief. Now no one plays with me at recess. And speaking of school, I HATE! HATE! HATE! school. I get into trouble a lot and get sent to the principal's office almost every day. The principal said he was going to suspend me if I didn't start behaving myself. I pretended like I didn't care, but I really felt bad. And I know my mom would totally freak out if I got suspended! She's already mad at me enough. We argue all the time. Last night, she wouldn't let me stay up late to watch the baseball game on TV so I threw the remote control at her and told her I wished she died instead of daddy. Later I felt bad about what I said. Maybe God will take away my mom to punish me for being so bad. I don't want my mom to die. And I wished my dad didn't die. I really miss my dad.

Something for Your Feel Better Bag:
Writing about My Feelings
(Supplies: Pencil)

When children get into trouble a lot, it's usually because they're upset and can't talk about their feelings. But when children start to talk more and more about what's really bothering them, they usually feel better and their behavior improves.

Add a pencil to your *Feel Better Bag*. Next time you are upset, use the pencil to fill in the sentences below. Writing about how you feel instead of getting into trouble will help you feel better about yourself.

I feel upset because:

Instead of getting into trouble I will calmly talk to _____ about my feelings.

Making My Special Person Proud

We all make mistakes and do things that make us feel bad. We wish we could go back in time and make all our mistakes go away, but this is impossible. Instead, we can focus on right now. There are things you can do *now* to be the kind of person that would make your special person proud of you. Fill in the sentences below:

An achievement or proud moment I can think about:

A good deed I can do for someone:

Something I can do to make my special person proud:

Next time you feel bad, look at this list as a reminder of all the good you do!

Wondering Why Bad Things Happen

There are many wonderful things that happen in the world each and every day. But sometimes, bad things happen, like when your special person died. You may wonder why bad things happen, especially to someone you care about. You may even think it was your fault. But bad things happen sometimes, and there isn't any good reason. You didn't make it happen by being bad, and you can't change it by being good. You may wonder why God lets bad things happen. Not even the smartest people in the whole wide world know the answer to this question. But one thing we do know is that we can make good things happen. We can make the world a better place. Draw a picture to show what you can do to make the world a better place.

The Heads or Tails Feelings Game
(Supplies: A quarter, tokens, bag filled with small prizes)

Let's play a game about feelings. It is called the *Heads or Tails Feelings Game*. To play, take turns flipping a coin. If the coin lands on heads, answer a question from the *Heads* list below. If the answer is correct, get 2 tokens. If the coin lands on tails, follow the instructions from the *Tails* list below, then get one token. Play until all the questions have been answered. At the end of the game, trade in tokens for prizes: 1-10 tokens = 1 prize, 11 or more tokens = 2 prizes.

Heads
1. Name three feelings children have when someone special dies.
2. What does grief mean?
3. True or False: Many people find it hard to feel sad when someone special dies because they are in shock.
4. True or False: After someone special dies, people may have a hard time believing that person is really dead.
5. True or False: When a family member dies, children may worry that they will die soon too.
6. What are some reasons why people blame themselves for someone's death?
7. True or False: Children shouldn't cry when someone dies because it makes them look like a cry baby.
8. Name three good ways to express anger.
9. Why do children often misbehave after someone in their family dies?
10. What can you do to feel better when you are upset?

Tails
1. Hop to the other end of the room and back on one foot.
2. Show what happy looks like with your face and body.
3. Spin your body around five times then try to touch your nose with your thumb.
4. Show what sad looks like with your face and body.
5. Jump up and down ten times.
6. Show what angry looks like with your face and body.
7. Do ten jumping jacks.
8. Show what scared looks like with your face and body.
9. Stomp your feet ten times.
10. Show what proud looks like with your face and body.

Answers to the Heads or Tails Feelings Game

1. Name three feelings children have when someone special dies: Children experience many different feelings when someone special dies, such as sad, scared, worried, confused, angry, guilty, and lonely.

2. What does grief mean? Grief means the sad, painful feelings we have when someone dies

3. True or False: Many people find it hard to feel sad when someone special dies because they are in shock. <u>True.</u> Some people are in shock when someone dies and they feel numb which means they feel nothing at all. For some people, it can take a long time before they are ready to feel the pain and sadness of grief.

4. True or False: After someone special dies, children may have a hard time believing that person is really dead. <u>True.</u> Some children think that their special person will come back to life because it is hard to accept that a person is dead and never coming back.

5. True or False: When a family member dies, children may worry that they will die soon too. <u>True.</u> When a family member dies, children may worry that they will die soon too. Although it is normal to feel this way, it is important to know that most people live a long and healthy life.

6. What are some reasons why people blame themselves for someone's death? Many people believe they caused their loved one to die because of something they thought, said, or wished. But it is important to know that people's words, wishes, and thoughts cannot make someone die.

7. True or False: Children shouldn't cry when someone dies because it makes them look like a cry baby. <u>False.</u> Crying is a strong, brave thing to do and it is a normal way to let out feelings.

8. Name three good ways to express anger. There are many ways to express anger in good ways, such as: Visualizing a stop sign, counting backwards, taking slow deep breaths, relaxing muscles, and talking to someone.

9. Why do children often misbehave after someone in their family dies? Sometimes children misbehave after someone dies because they feel so upset. They find it hard to talk about their upset feelings so they show they are upset by misbehaving. But when children start to talk more about what's bothering them, they usually feel better and their behavior improves.

10. What can you do to feel better when you are upset? There are many ways we can help ourselves feel better when we are upset. For example, we can write or draw about our feelings, or talk to someone.

Section 6

Interventions to Help Children Understand Death

One of the key tasks of mourning is helping children understand death and its finality. Another important task of mourning is for children to engage in grieving rituals. The interventions in this section facilitate these tasks. Care must be taken to respect the child and family's cultural and religious beliefs about death and mourning. The practitioner can ask about the family's beliefs while collecting information during the assessment.

Interventions

Life and Death, About Death, What Causes Death, What Happens After Death: These interventions educate children about death, counter any misconceptions they have about death, and help children talk more freely about death. Children are introduced to basic death concepts, such as, "what it means to be dead," "death is not contagious," and "death is irreversible." The activity, *What Happens After Death* defines terms such as cemetery, coffin, and urn, and helps children explore their beliefs of what happens after death. This activity can be modified for older children by having them draw a coffin and urn, rather than coloring in the existing picture.

The Funeral: The story, *The Zebra's Funeral,* normalizes grief reactions and helps children explore and process issues such as, the finality of death, magical thinking, and eulogizing the dead. The worksheet helps the child identify thoughts and feelings about the funeral.

Basketball: A Game About Life and Death: This game helps children integrate the concepts that were covered in the preceding activities on death and grieving rituals. Modifying the traditional game of basketball can engage otherwise resistant children. Blank cards can be added so clients can make up their own questions for the game.

Life and Death

Today we are going to talk about what it means to be alive, and what it means to be dead. All living things grow and change and eventually die. Death is natural and everything that lives eventually dies. Plants die, animals die, and people die. Death happens when a person's body becomes so old, sick or injured that it stops working and breathing. Complete the following exercises to understand the difference between being alive and being dead:

Take a deep breath and let it out. You are alive, which means you are breathing. When a person is dead, they do not breathe.

Put your hand on your heart and feel it beating. You are alive, which means your heart is beating. When a person is dead, the heart stops beating.

Blink your eyes three times. You are alive, which means you can blink your eyes. When a person is dead, they cannot blink their eyes.

Pinch your arm (not too hard!) You are alive, which means you can hurt and feel pain. When a person is dead they do not hurt or feel pain.

Do five jumping jacks. You are alive, which means you can move. When a person is dead they cannot move their body.

When someone or something is <u>alive</u>, it can move, breathe, and feel. Draw a picture of an animal, insect, plant, or person that is alive:

When someone or something is <u>dead</u>, it cannot move, breathe, or feel anything. Draw a picture of an animal, insect, plant, or person that is dead:

About Death Puzzle
(Supplies: Scissors, tape)

It can feel scary or weird talking about death, so let's do a puzzle to make it easier. Prepare the puzzle by cutting along the dotted lines below. Then pick one puzzle piece at a time, in order from one to six, and follow the instructions. Once you have completed all six puzzle pieces, put the puzzle together and put it in this book.

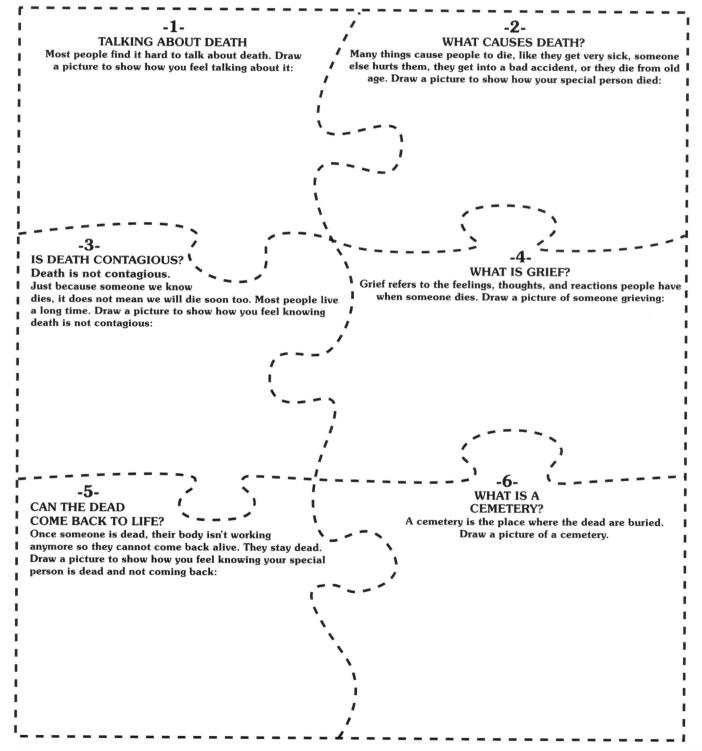

-1-
TALKING ABOUT DEATH
Most people find it hard to talk about death. Draw a picture to show how you feel talking about it:

-2-
WHAT CAUSES DEATH?
Many things cause people to die, like they get very sick, someone else hurts them, they get into a bad accident, or they die from old age. Draw a picture to show how your special person died:

-3-
IS DEATH CONTAGIOUS?
Death is not contagious. Just because someone we know dies, it does not mean we will die soon too. Most people live a long time. Draw a picture to show how you feel knowing death is not contagious:

-4-
WHAT IS GRIEF?
Grief refers to the feelings, thoughts, and reactions people have when someone dies. Draw a picture of someone grieving:

-5-
CAN THE DEAD COME BACK TO LIFE?
Once someone is dead, their body isn't working anymore so they cannot come back alive. They stay dead. Draw a picture to show how you feel knowing your special person is dead and not coming back:

-6-
WHAT IS A CEMETERY?
A cemetery is the place where the dead are buried. Draw a picture of a cemetery.

Something for Your Feel Better Bag: Wonderful Things in Life

Make a list of some things that are alive that you really like or think are really great—like a newborn kitten, a beautiful colored butterfly, or a child laughing and playing in the park. Add your list to your *Feel Better Bag*. When you look at your list, it will help remind you of the wonderful things in life that can make you feel good!

What Causes Death

All living things die. Plants die, animals die, and people die. There are many different causes of death. But people's words or thoughts never cause death. Even though you might feel like you caused your special person to die, people's words, thoughts, and wishes cannot cause death. Nothing you said, thought, or did made your special person die. This activity will help you understand what causes death. Below is a list of things that can cause death. Some can cause death and some cannot. Read each one and put an "X" under "Yes" if you think it can cause death, and put an "X" under "No" if you think it cannot cause death. (The answers are on the next page.) If there are words you do not understand, ask your therapist to explain.

Things that can cause death	Yes	No
Being hit by a car		
Cancer		
Saying to someone, "I hate you, I wish you were dead!"		
Getting shot with a gun		
Getting bad grades at school		
Taking an overdose of drugs		
War		
Shouting at your parents		
Suicide		
Thinking mean thoughts about someone		
Tornadoes		
Making a mess in your room		
Feeling angry at someone		
Terrorist attack		
Wishing someone dead		

Answers: What Causes Death

Things that can cause death	Yes	No
Being hit by a car	X	
Cancer	X	
Saying to someone, "I hate you, I wish you were dead!"		X
Getting shot with a gun	X	
Getting bad grades at school		X
Taking an overdose of drugs	X	
War	X	
Shouting at your parents		X
Suicide	X	
Thinking mean thoughts about someone		X
Tornadoes	X	
Making a mess in your room		X
Feeling angry at someone		X
Terrorist attack	X	
Wishing someone dead		X

Explanations of What Causes Death:

Accidents, like being hit by a car, can cause death.

Certain illnesses can cause death, like cancer or AIDS. If these illnesses are not treated with strong medicine, they can cause death. Sometimes even the best medicine doesn't help. The illness makes the person's body stop working and the person dies.

There are illnesses in the brain, called mental illnesses, which can cause death. Depression is a mental illness. People with depression may feel so sad and hopeless that they think it would be better to die than to go on living. So they may kill themselves. This kind of death is called suicide.

Sometimes a person kills another person on purpose. This kind of death is called murder or homicide. Sometimes people kill other people like in a war or terrorist attack. A terrorist attack is a surprise attack by one person or a group of people on other people usually for political reasons.

Natural disasters, like hurricanes, tornadoes, or tsunamis, can cause death.

Our words, feelings, wishes, or thoughts do not cause death.

Something for Your Feel Better Bag: I Feel Good Knowing I Didn't Make My Special Person Die

There was a cause to your special person's death, but it was not anything you said or thought. Draw a picture of yourself to show how you feel knowing that nothing you said or thought made your special person die. Add your picture to your *Feel Better Bag* as a reminder that you did not make your special person die.

What Happens After Death

People from different religions have their own special way of taking care of their dead. Some people believe that washing and dressing the person who died is very important. The dead body may be placed in a coffin or casket. This is a large wooden or steel box that holds the person who died. When a dead body is placed in a coffin or casket, the person's eyes and mouth are closed, and they look like they are asleep, but they are not. Color in the picture of the coffin below:

After a person dies, his or her body is either buried in the ground, or cremated. Cremation means the body is burned into ashes. Being buried in the ground or cremated may seem weird, scary or gross, but the person who died cannot feel anything. It doesn't hurt even a bit because dead bodies do not feel any pain. After the body is cremated, the ashes are buried in the ground, scattered in a special place, or kept at home in a special container called an urn. Color in the picture of the urn below:

People have different beliefs about what happens after death. Some people believe the spirit or soul goes to heaven or hell. Some believe in reincarnation (the dead come back to earth in a different body). Some believe there is a place where someone's spirit waits before joining God. Others are not sure what happens. Write or draw a picture to show what you think happens after death:

Something for Your Feel Better Bag: Drink Something Warm and Soothing

(Supplies: Packet of hot chocolate mix)

Drinking something warm is very soothing and can help you relax when you are upset. Add the packet of hot chocolate to your *Feel Better Bag*. Next time you are feeling upset about your special person's death, make a cup of hot chocolate (ask an adult to help you). While you are drinking it, take slow deep breaths and allow yourself to relax. Feel how calm and relaxed it makes your body feel.

The Funeral

(Supplies: Plastic jungle animals, ready or home-made funeral props, i.e. casket, tombstone, flowers, etc.)

A funeral is when family and friends come together to say goodbye to the person who died and to remember the good things about the dead person. Sometimes the dead body is there to see or to touch if anyone wants to. *The Zebra's Funeral* is a story to help you understand about death and funerals. Have your therapist read the story while you act it out with plastic animals. Then answer the questions below:

Describe the funeral the animals planned for their friend the zebra:

What do you remember about your special person's funeral?

Did you see the body of your special person after s/he died? What was that like?

Were you there when your special person's body was buried (or cremated)? How did you feel about that?

What did you feel at the funeral and were you able to show your true feelings?

Write what you remember about the eulogy, or what people said about your special person at his/her funeral:

Is there anything you wished was different about the funeral? Write about it:

The Zebra's Funeral

Once upon a time, in a far away jungle, there lived some animals; an elephant, a giraffe, a lion, tiger, and zebra. The jungle animals used to be enemies and hunt and chase each other. But one day they decided to become friends so they could all be safe and live happily ever after. They shared their food, they laughed and played together, and they protected one another from danger. The animals were happy and became close friends. Then one day, something terrible happened. The zebra died.

At first, the animals could not believe their friend the zebra had died. They thought, maybe if we act really good all day, the zebra will come back. But the next day, the zebra was still dead. The lion was angry that his friend the zebra was dead and let out a mighty roar! The giraffe said, "Our friend the zebra is dead and gone forever. It is very sad. We must plan a funeral." "What's a funeral?" asked the elephant. "A funeral is a special ceremony where everyone comes to honor and remember the dead." So the jungle animals gathered together for the zebra's funeral. They played special music and placed flowers all around. "What's that box the zebra is lying in?" asked the tiger. The giraffe replied, "It's a special wooden box called a casket." The elephant walked over to the casket and saw the zebra lying in it. "Our friend the zebra is not dead, he is just asleep!" said the elephant with excitement. The giraffe said, "Our friend the zebra looks like he is sleeping, because his eyes are closed and he is not moving. But I am sad to say that he is dead. His body stopped working. He can no longer eat or sleep, talk or breathe or feel anything. Now it is time to honor and remember our friend the zebra who died. Lion, since you are the king of the jungle, why don't you do the Eulogy." "What's a Eulogy?" asked the lion. The giraffe responded, "It is a speech made about the dead to honor his or her life." And so the lion made a speech about his friend the zebra. He talked about what a good friend the zebra was, how he was nice to everyone, even to the flies who were such a nuisance! He mentioned the zebra's special ability to run long distances, and he talked about how the zebra will be missed by all his friends in the jungle. The animals listened carefully to the lion's eulogy. The elephant and the giraffe cried, and the tiger laughed—not because he was happy, but because he felt uncomfortable and did not know what else to do.

Then it was time to bury the zebra. The animals carefully carried the zebra in his casket to the grave site, the beautiful spot near the waterfall, where the zebra loved to visit. The giraffe closed the lid of the casket, and the animals lowered the wooden casket holding their friend the zebra into the ground. The giraffe threw some earth over the casket to bury it. "Stop!" cried out the elephant. "If you put our friend the zebra into the ground and bury him, he won't be able to breathe and he will feel scared." "Don't worry," said the giraffe, "Remember what I said earlier. When a body dies, it stops working. It can no longer breathe or feel any pain. So it won't hurt our friend the zebra to be in the box buried in the ground." All the animals breathed a sigh of relief.

The giraffe placed a tombstone by the grave. "What's that?" asked the lion. "It's a tombstone. It has our friend the zebra's name, the day he was born, and the day he died. I am placing it on the grave so we know where our friend the zebra is buried and we can come back whenever we want and visit the grave." The animals placed flowers on top of the grave where their friend the zebra was buried.

Although it was a sad day, and the animals knew they would miss their friend the zebra, it helped to know that they could return to the grave site whenever they wanted, and place flowers on top of the grave, and this would help them remember their special friend the zebra.

Something for Your Feel Better Bag: Death Dictionary

Below is a dictionary of words we have been talking about. Add the dictionary to your *Feel Better Bag* so you can look up a word when you need to. Add any other words you don't understand and ask an adult helper to explain what they mean.

Death Dictionary

Dead: When a person's body becomes so old, sick, or injured that it stops working and breathing

Grief: Feelings, thoughts, and reactions people have when someone dies

Funeral: A ceremony to honor and remember the person who died

Funeral Home: The place where people go to attend a funeral

Mortician/Funeral Director: The person who prepares the dead person for the funeral. For example, cleans the body, dresses and does the dead person's hair.

Coffin/Casket: A wooden or steel box that holds the body of the person who died

Cremation: When a dead body is burned in very high heat and turned to ashes. Since a dead body does not feel any pain, cremation does not hurt

Urn: A container that holds the ashes of the person who died after the body has been cremated

Cemetery/Grave: The place where dead people are buried

Mausoleum: A special building or tomb that holds the dead body

Obituary: An announcement in the newspaper telling about a person's death

Eulogy: A speech made about the person who died to honor his or her life

Tombstone: A stone that is put on the grave where the dead person is buried. It usually has the dead person's name, year they were born, and year they died. Other things may be put on a tombstone like a prayer or special saying, even a picture.

Memory: Something you remember about the person who died or something you did with them.

Basketball: A Game about Life and Death
(Supplies: Basketball hoop and ball, <u>or</u> crumpled paper and garbage can, tokens, bag filled with prizes)

It can be hard to talk about death, so let's play a special version of *Basketball* to make it easier. To play, take turns shooting a basket. If you successfully throw the ball through the basketball hoop, you get two tokens. If you miss the basket, answer one of the questions below. You get one token for each question you answer. At the end of the game, trade in tokens for prizes: 1-10 tokens = 1 prize, 11 or more tokens = 2 prizes.

-1- True or False: Most people find it hard to talk about death.	**-2-** True or False: Every living thing eventually dies.
-3- What are some things that cause death?	**-4-** Name three things that happen to a person's body when they die.
-5- What is a casket?	**-6-** What is an urn?
-7- True or False: When a dead person is cremated or buried, they feel scared because they don't like being burned or put in the ground.	**-8-** If someone in your family dies, does that mean that you will die soon too?
-9- Can a dead person come back alive?	**-10-** True or False: Everyone feels sad and cries when someone in their family dies.
-11- True or False: Only old people die.	**-12-** True or False: Even though your special person died, you can still be happy, laugh, and play.

Answers to Basketball Game

1. True or False: Most people find it hard to talk about death. <u>True</u>: Death can be hard to talk about, but the more you talk about it, the easier it gets.

2. True or False: Every living thing eventually dies. <u>True.</u> Death is natural and everything that lives eventually dies. Plants die. Animals die. People die.

3. What are some things that cause death? People die for different reasons. They get into an accident, get sick, get killed or kill themselves, or they die of old age.

4. Name three things that happen to a person's body when they die. When a person dies, their body stops working. The heart stops beating, the person stops breathing, they don't blink their eyes, they stop growing, and they don't feel any pain.

5. What is a casket? A casket is a wooden or steel box that holds the body of the person who died. It is sometimes called a coffin.

6. What is an urn? An urn is a container that holds the ashes of the person who died after the body has been cremated.

7. True or False: When a dead person is cremated or buried, they feel scared because they don't like being burned or put in the ground. <u>False.</u> Although it may seem strange or scary to cremate someone or bury them in the ground, it doesn't hurt to be cremated or buried because once someone is dead, they cannot feel anything. They do not feel scared, and they do not feel any pain.

8. If someone in your family dies, does that mean that you will die soon too? No. Most people live a long time and die when they are old.

9. Can a dead person come back alive? No, even if we wish really hard, when a body dies it stops working forever, and so it cannot come back alive again.

10. True or False: Everyone feels sad and cries when someone in their family dies. <u>False.</u> People have different reactions when someone dies. Some people feel sad, and some people don't feel anything at all. Some cry, and some don't. Some people are in shock, which means they find it hard to feel anything at all.

11. True or False: Only old people die. <u>False.</u> People of all ages die. Babies, children, teenagers, adults, and elderly people die. It is very sad when someone young dies. Most people live a long and healthy life.

12. True or False: Even though your special person died, you can still be happy, laugh, and play. <u>True.</u> Even though you may feel very sad about your special person's death, you can still feel happy, laugh, and play. There may be times when you feel sad, and other times when you feel happy. All your feelings are normal and okay.

Section 7

Interventions to Commemorate the Deceased

Children need to be able to remember and memorialize the deceased person, not only after the death but throughout their later years. Reminiscing about the deceased and looking at photographs and other special objects that belonged to the person who died can help children memorialize the person who has died. The interventions in this section facilitate this process.

Interventions

My Special Person, Memory Tape, A Penny for Your Thoughts, Keepsakes: These activities help children document memories and commemorate the deceased. Young children may have difficulty recalling memories, so it can be helpful to have children look at photographs of themselves with the deceased, or ask family members to assist in recalling memories.

What I Liked and Didn't Like: Children often focus only on positive memories of the dead, fearing that speaking negatively of the dead will have detrimental consequences. However, an important treatment goal with bereaved children is to process ambivalent feelings toward the deceased. This activity facilitates this goal. It should be completed before the other commemorative activities in this section, so that the child can process negative memories, before documenting positive memories of the deceased.

I Wish My Special Person Was Still Alive: Many children yearn for the deceased person. Some children experience "magical thinking" in that they believe they have the power to bring the deceased person back. Once they realize the person is not coming back, they often feel overwhelmingly sad and powerless. This activity normalizes the sense of loss, reinforces the finality of the death, and empowers children to focus on the positive.

Saying Goodbye: Some children will not have had a chance to say goodbye to the person before they died. Writing a letter to the deceased guides children through the goodbye process, and helps them resolve any "unfinished business" they may have with the deceased person. The sentence completion provides structure to the letter and directs children toward specific issues they may not otherwise bring up on their own.

My Special Person

A memory is something we remember about something or someone. When a special person dies, we can no longer see them or touch them, but we can remember them. It's important to talk about people after they have died so we don't forget them. Writing and drawing about your special person who died will help you remember. Draw a picture or paste a photo of your special person below:

Fill in the sentences below about your special person who died. If you are unsure of some of the answers, be a detective and see if you can find out more about him or her.

My special person was born on _____. He/she was born in _____

My special person liked to_____

My special person's favorite food was _____

My special person's hobbies were _____

Other important information about my special person _____

_____

_____

_____

_____

Something for Your Feel Better Bag:
Always in My Heart

Cut out the heart below, draw a picture of your special person inside the heart and decorate the heart. Add the heart to your *Feel Better Bag*. Let it remind you that your special person who died is always in your heart!

What I Liked and Didn't Like

Nobody is perfect, not even your special person who died. Chances are there are things you liked and didn't like about the person who died. Fill in the questions below and draw a sad face beside the things you didn't like, and draw a happy face beside the things you liked about your special person.

What I Didn't Like:

◯ Something my special person did that bothered or upset me:

◯ A mistake my special person made:

◯ A sad memory of my special person:

What I Liked:

◯ Something my special person did that made me happy:

◯ Something my special person taught me:

◯ A happy memory of my special person:

Something for Your Feel Better Bag: Happy Times

Draw a happy face below and add it to your *Feel Better Bag*. Let it be a reminder of the happy times you shared with your special person. Remember that even though your special person is dead, your happy memories will live on forever!

Memory Tape
(Supplies: Tape recorder or video recorder)

You shared many times with your special person before he or she died. It is important to capture these memories so you don't forget them. Video or tape record yourself talking about your memories. Below is a guide you may want to follow. It may help to write down your memories before you record them. Keep your tape at home in a safe, private place. Listen to it every once in a while—it will help keep your memories alive forever!

1. Begin by telling who your special person was and what s/he meant to you

2. Describe in as much detail as possible what your special person looked like

3. Record some of your memories. Here are some ideas of what to include:

• Your earliest memory of your special person

• Holidays, birthdays, trips, or other special celebrations

• Funny moments spent with your special person

• Things your special person used to say

• Times you and your special person hugged or cuddled together

• Special moments when you made your special person proud

• Favorite gifts you gave or received from your special person

• Nicest thing the person ever did for you

4. End by talking about your best time with your special person

A Penny for Your Thoughts
(Supplies: Penny, bag filled with small prizes)

This game is called *A Penny for Your Thoughts*. It is a game to help you share memories of your special person who died. To play, toss a penny onto this page and follow the instructions. If the penny lands on a question you have already answered, toss the penny again until it lands on a new square. (Check off the questions you have answered to help yourself keep track.)

What is a memory?	Tell about a happy memory with your special person	Get a prize!	Tell about a holiday spent with your special person
Tell about a meal shared with your special person	Give a prize to someone else in the room	Tell about a gift you gave your special person	Tell how you feel when you look at photos of your special person
Tell about a funny moment with your special person	Get a prize!	Tell about a sad memory with your special person	Tell about a trip or outing with your special person
Give a prize to someone else in the room	Why is it important to talk about memories of someone who died?	Tell about a gift your special person gave you	Tell about the last time you saw your special person

Keepsakes

Keepsakes are items that you have that remind you of your special person who died. They may be items that belonged to your special person and that were passed on to you, or they may be things around your home that remind you of your special person. In the space below, write about, draw a picture, or paste photos of these special keepsakes. Describe why they are important to you.

You may wish to make a memory box for your keepsakes. Use a strong sturdy box or plastic bin. You can decorate the box and paste photos of your special person on the lid. Fill your box with your keepsakes. If any keepsakes are too large for the box, take a photo of them and place the photos in the box. When you look through your keepsake box, it will bring back memories and help you feel close to your special person.

Something for Your Feel Better Bag: Keepsake

Keep something that belonged to your special person in your *Feel Better Bag* (or a photo of a special keepsake). Every once in a while, look at it, touch it, and remember your special person. Always remember that even though your special person has died, your memories will last forever and ever!

I Wish My Special Person Was Still Alive

It is normal to wish for your special person to come back alive. Many children wish for this more than anything. The story, *Willy's Wishes and the Wise Wizard*, will help you talk about these feelings. Read the story then answer the questions below.

How did Willy feel after his mother died?

What special power does Willy (and each and every person) have? How does this special power help Willy?

Make a list of things that you do have:

Willy's Wishes and the Wise Wizard

This is a story about a boy named Willy. His real name is William but most people call him Willy. Willy was a typical kid; he liked to play computer games and ride his bike, and he preferred dessert to eating vegetables!

Willy led a pretty normal, happy life until something awful happened…his mother died. Then his whole life changed. He felt terribly sad, scared, and lonely, but he did not want to talk about these feelings with anyone. Because of all his sad, scared, and lonely feelings, Willy sometimes did things he never used to, like getting mad at people for no good reason. Often he had a nervous feeling that would give him stomachaches. Night time was especially difficult because he had a hard time falling asleep, and he often had scary dreams. And sometimes he would wet his bed.

Willy stopped laughing and playing and having fun. He spent much of his time in his secret hiding spot, curled up in a little ball. He would lie there for hours and think about how much better things would be if his mother were still alive.

One day, while at his secret hiding spot, he fell asleep and dreamed the most wonderful dream—that he had magical powers and could make wishes come true! So, he wished for a new shiny red bike, and for chocolate fudge cake for dessert every day, and for his mother to come back alive—and poof! His wishes came true! He felt so happy! But then something startled him, and he woke up and realized it was just a dream. No new shiny red bike. No chocolate fudge cake for dessert every day. And worst of all, his mother had not come back alive. He felt so sad. He buried his head in his teddy bear and cried. He lay there for a long time, and after a while, he fell asleep again. This time, he dreamed that a wizard came to him—a very old, wise wizard, named Waldorf. He had a long white beard, and he wore a long purple cape with bright yellow shiny stars and a tall pointy hat to match. But he did not have a magic wand. "You can't be a real wizard," said Willy, "because you do not have a magic wand." "Oh, but you see, my boy, I do not need a magic wand, for I have discovered a special power that does not require any magic." "What kind of special power?" asked Willy. "Well," replied Waldorf the Wizard, "It is a special power that will bring you happiness. It is the power to think about all that you have." "Huh, what do you mean?" asked Willy. "Well, instead of thinking about what you *do not* have, think about what you *do* have. And if you think about all that you have, this will bring you happiness." "I wish I had that special power," said Willy. "Ah, but you do have this special power," replied Waldorf. "In fact, each and *every* person has this special power. They just have to use it." "So you mean I have this special power?" asked Willy. "Yes! I'll show you what I mean. First think about what you do not have." "Well," said Willy, "I do not have a new shiny red bike. And I do not get to eat chocolate fudge cake for dessert every day. And worst of all, I do not have a mother." "And how do you feel when you think about what you do not have?" "I feel sad" replied Willy. "Now, think about what you *do* have." "Well, let's see, I have a bike that I got two years ago and it has a cool yellow banana seat that the kids on my street think is pretty neat. And I get chocolate fudge cake sometimes, like when it's my birthday. And I have a family that cares about me." "How do you feel now, as you think about what you do have?" "I feel better!" replied Willy with a smile on his face. "You see! You have the power to think about what you *do* have, and if you choose to use this power, you will feel better!" Just then, something startled Willy, and he woke up from his dream. He ran to his room and got a pen and paper. He made a list of all that he had. And whenever he started to feel sad, scared, and lonely, he looked at his list, and this made him feel better. Wow! He thought to himself, I do have special power!

Something for Your Feel Better Bag: Feeling Happy for All That I Have

Look at the list of things that you *do* have. Choose three things from this list and write them below. Next time you feel upset, look at this list. And remember Waldorf the Wizard's message…if you think about what you do have, you will feel happier!

Saying Goodbye

You may not have had a chance to say goodbye to your special person, or there may be things you wished you had said before your special person died. It can be helpful to write a letter to the person who has died. Complete the letter below or write your own to express the things you never had a chance to say:

Dear _____

Since your death I have been feeling _____

And I want you to know that _____

_____

_____

I am really glad that we _____

I am sorry that we never had a chance to _____

_____ . *I will miss never being*

able to _____ *with you ever again. I feel*

sad that you won't be there when I _____

and this makes me feel _____

What I miss most is _____

If you were here now I would tell you _____

I think if you were here now you would tell me _____

I feel good knowing that _____

One day I will tell my children that you were _____

_____

Thank you for _____

Love,

_____

Talk with your therapist about what you would like to do with your letter. For example, you could record it on tape, or go to your special person's grave and read it aloud, or bury it in the ground, or place a picture of your special person on a chair and read it to him/her.

Something for Your Feel Better Bag:
Sympathy Cards
(Supplies: Sympathy cards)

A sympathy card is a card that someone sends to a person who is grieving, to let them know they care and to offer them words of comfort. Write a sympathy card to yourself, and have your therapist write one to you as well. Add the cards to your *Feel Better Bag*. Read the cards when you need comfort.

Section 8

Interventions to Enhance Coping and Self-Esteem

Many bereaved children use maladaptive strategies to cope with their grief. If children do not learn healthy ways to cope, they are at risk for developing serious difficulties, such as depression, anxiety, or anti-social behavior. A number of interventions in this section focus on enhancing coping strategies.

A significant loss can damage a child's self-esteem. Some children have such profound self-esteem deficits that they have internalized the belief that they are bad and their future is hopeless. Enhancing self-esteem for these children is not easy, yet is essential in helping the child be resilient and able to cope with adversity in life. Activities from this section are designed to improve children's self-esteem, and encourage a positive view of their future. In order to strengthen a child's self-concept, caregivers must be part of the process and must be coached how to positively interact with their children and foster their children's unique talents. The activities in this section will be significantly enhanced by working in conjunction with caregivers.

Interventions

Feeling Good About Myself, Something Good Can Come From This, I Deserve To Be Happy and Enjoy Life, Feel Good Messages: These activities can be used as tools to help children focus on their strengths and abilities, promote feelings of self-worth, encourage a more optimistic attitude, and instill a message of hope for the future.

Making My Bad Dreams Better, Helping Myself When I Have Scary Thoughts: Many bereaved children suffer from nightmares or frightening intrusive thoughts. If nightmares or intrusive thoughts are interfering with the child's daily functioning, these activities can be used in the earlier stages of therapy.

Coping with Grief Attacks: It is important to prepare children for the likelihood that painful feelings will be reactivated at different times in the future, such as the anniversary of the death. A variety of ideas are presented to help children cope with "grief attacks."

The Coping with Grief Game: This game helps children integrate the many concepts addressed throughout the interventions in this book. It facilitates the child's problem-solving abilities, which is an important goal in the final stages of therapy.

Giving A Helping Hand, What I Learned: These interventions are used at the end of therapy. *Giving A Helping Hand* provides children with the opportunity to offer words of advice to other grieving children. This is very empowering. *What I Learned* helps children review and evaluate their experiences in therapy. To prepare the activity, select a small gift appropriate to the client, for example, a small stuffed animal, or bottle of bubble bath. The gift can also be a graduation certificate, or the child's scrapbook. The gift should be wrapped in five layers of different colored wrapping or tissue paper so that each time the child answers one of the five questions on the worksheet, s/he gets to unwrap one layer of the gift.

Looking At This Book: This activity should be done in the second to last session. It helps the child review achievements in therapy, and prepares the child to share his or her scrapbook with his or her caregivers. If the child chooses to share the book with caregivers, it is suggested that the practitioner meet with the caregivers ahead of time to prepare them to respond appropriately to the child and the material in the scrapbook. This activity facilitates parent/child dialogue regarding the importance of keeping the book in a safe, private place.

Feeling Good About Myself:
The Balloon Bounce Game
(Supplies: 6 balloons)

Today we are going to talk about self-esteem. Self-esteem means how you feel about yourself. If you have good feelings about yourself, it means you have high self-esteem. You can help yourself have high self-esteem by thinking about the good things, like things you do well and your proud moments. The *Balloon Bounce Game* will help us talk about these good things. To play, blow up six balloons and knot each one. Write one question from the list below onto each balloon. (Use a pen as markers will smudge.) Now try to keep two balloons up in the air for one minute without them touching the ground. Then catch a balloon, read the question written on it, and take turns answering the question. Repeat until all questions have been answered. At the end, you can burst the balloons!

Questions

What's something you are proud you can do?

Tell about a time you were able to do something difficult

Tell about a time you felt proud of yourself

Tell about a time you were nice to someone

Tell about a time you helped yourself feel better

Say something nice to someone else in the room

Something for Your Feel Better Bag: My Proud Moment

(Supplies: Balloon)

Fill in the sentence below:

Something I did that I'm especially proud of_____

_____

Put a balloon in your *Feel Better Bag.* **Next time you are feeling upset, blow up the balloon, tie it, and bounce it in the air without letting it touch the ground for as long as you can. As you are bouncing the balloon, think about your proud moment that you wrote about in the space above.**

Coping With Bad Dreams
(Supplies: White pillowcase, fabric markers)

Everyone has bad dreams sometimes. In the space below, draw a picture of a bad dream you have had recently:

Below are things you can do to help yourself when you wake up from a bad dream. Choose one of the strategies and write or draw it on a pillow case. Take the pillowcase home and put it on your pillow or next to your bed. Next time you wake up during the night from a bad dream, the pillowcase will remind you to use your strategy!

Say to myself: It's not real, it's just a dream

Think of a happy ending to the dream

Imagine my favorite superhero fighting off the scary monsters

Hug my pillow or stuffed animal until I feel calm and safe

Think about a happy memory

Helping Myself When I Have Scary Thoughts
(Supplies: Happy face stickers)

You may have scary thoughts or memories about your special person's death. Sometimes these scary thoughts or memories come, even if you don't want them to. Draw or write about your scary thoughts or scary memories in the space below:

There are things you can do to help yourself when you get these scary thoughts or memories. Put a happy face sticker beside the ones you think would help you:

Tell an adult who will listen to you about the scary thoughts or memories

Imagine a safe, happy place, and pretend that you are there

Think about a good memory

When you have these scary thoughts, think and say to yourself "Stop!"

Repeat to yourself, "I am safe now"

Imagine your favorite superhero fighting off the scary thoughts or memories

Start doing something you enjoy

Something for Your Feel Better Bag: Coping With Scary Thoughts

There are many ways you can help yourself when you have scary thoughts. Choose one of the coping techniques from the list on the previous page. Draw a picture of yourself using this idea. Add the picture to your *Feel Better Bag* as a reminder to use the technique when you have scary thoughts or memories.

Something Good Can Come From This
(Supplies: Cup, spoon, lemon, sugar, water)

You may wonder why your special person had to die. Unfortunately, there are no easy answers to this difficult question. Sometimes bad things happen to people we care about, and we don't know why. But one thing you can do is to think about something good that can come from the person's death. This may be hard to do at first, but thinking positive thoughts or helping others will help you feel better. For example, you could donate to a charity or do a good deed, in honor of your special person who died. What can you do to turn the tragedy of your special person's death into something good? Write your ideas in the space below:

When someone turns a bad situation into something good, it is called "Turning lemons into lemonade." This is because someone is taking something bad or sour (like lemons) and making them into something good (like lemonade). Follow the recipe below to make lemonade. As you are drinking the lemonade, read about some famous people below who turned their bad situation into something good (people who turned lemons into lemonade).

Lemonade: Squeeze the juice from 1 lemon into a cup. Add half a cup of sugar. Add water to taste.

Famous people who turned lemons into lemonade

Terry Fox got bone cancer when he was 18 and his right leg had to be amputated. Even though he only had one good leg, he ran across Canada to raise money for cancer research. After running for 143 days, he had to stop because he became too sick. He died a few months later. The Terry Fox Marathon is held around the world each year and millions of dollars are raised in his name.

Candy Lightner and a group of other mothers founded MADD (Mothers Against Drunk Driving) in 1980 after a teenage girl was killed by a drunk driver. MADD has grown to include groups all over the country who dedicate time to ending drunk driving.

Mattie Stepanek was a boy who had a disease that prevented him from walking or breathing properly. He died at the age of 14, but before he died, he wrote five books of poems about world peace.

Something for Your Feel Better Bag: Lemonade

Put the recipe for lemonade in your *Feel Better Bag* as a reminder that turning lemons into lemonade is a way to help yourself feel better.

<u>**Lemonade**</u>

Squeeze the juice from 1 lemon into a cup
Add half a cup of sugar
Add water to taste

I Deserve To Be Happy And Enjoy Life!
(Supplies: Marshmallows, pretzel sticks, icing)

You have been through a sad time since your special person died, and you may have stopped doing things you enjoy. It may seem difficult to play, laugh, or have fun now, but you can--and you deserve to. You can be happy and enjoy life! Write down three things you like doing:

I like to _____

I like to _____

I like to _____

Make a marshmallow person. Use marshmallows for the head and body and pretzel sticks for the arms and legs. Use icing for the face and hair.

Pretend the marshmallow person is you. Use the marshmallow person to make a skit showing yourself doing something you really enjoy. (When you are done, you can eat your marshmallow person!)

Make a plan to do something you enjoy this week. If it's something that you used to do with your special person, you can feel good about the happy memories you have!

Something for Your Feel Better Bag:
Things I Enjoy

Next time you are feeling upset, try this strategy: Close your eyes and think about the things you enjoy doing. Let the happy feelings spread through your body. Just thinking about the things you enjoy doing can bring you happiness!

Coping With Grief Attacks
(Supplies: Calendar)

Your sadness about your special person's death will come and go. There will be times when you feel good and other times when you feel sad. Even long after the death, certain things will remind you of your special person, and this may make you feel sad. These are called grief attacks. Holidays or other special occasions may be particularly difficult, because you will wish your special person could be with you. But if you plan ahead, there are things you can do to get yourself through these grief attacks. Circle on the calendar the days of the year you think will be more difficult for you. Then on each of those days, write down something you can do to help yourself feel better. Below are some ideas:

Honor your special person's memory on the anniversary of his or her death, i.e. look at family photos, eat your special person's favorite food, participate in one of your special person's favorite activities, etc.

You can still celebrate your special person's birthday even though s/he is dead. Honor your special person by making him or her a birthday card and eating birthday cake. You can even blow out candles and make a birthday wish on behalf of your special person!

On your birthday, write down or draw a picture of a special memory you shared with your special person. Let this memory be a gift you give to yourself each year.

If your special person who died was a parent, then Mother's Day/Father's Day will be hard. You may feel sad, lonely, jealous, or angry on this day, especially when you see other children with their parents. Even though your mother or father has died, he or she is still your parent and you may want to honor him or her by making a Mother's/Father's Day card. You can visit the cemetery and leave the card at the grave or keep it in a special place.

Other times that may be difficult include holidays, family celebrations, graduations, etc. These are supposed to be happy times, but you may feel a mix of emotions because you miss the person who died. Remind yourself it is normal to experience both happy and sad feelings on these days, and think of ways you can help yourself and get comfort from others. For example, you can use a coping strategy from your *Feel Better Bag*, or look at this book as a reminder that you have made it through tough times. It can also be helpful to say to yourself, "I miss my special person but I'm going to be okay."

Feel Good Messages
(Supplies: Scissors, glue, colored paper, decorating materials)

Dealing with someone's death is sad and difficult, but there are things you can do to make it easier. Reading *Feel Good Messages* is one way you can help yourself feel better. Read the *Feel Good Messages* below, cut out the ones you find helpful and glue them onto colored paper. You can make up your own *Feel Good Messages* if you'd like. Decorate your poster and add it to your *Feel Better Bag*. Read the poster to yourself whenever you need help and comfort.

There are things I can do to help myself feel better

I made it through tough times before and I can make it through tough times now

Nothing I said or did caused my special person's death

I can feel good about my proud moments

I am strong and healthy

My special person has died but my memories of him or her will last forever

I am loved

I can be happy for all that I have

Even though my special person died, I can still be happy and enjoy life

The Coping with Grief Game
(Supplies: Bag filled with small prizes)

The Coping with Grief Game **will give you some ideas on how to cope better with your special person's death. To play the game, take turns reading the questions below, and circling the best answer (answers are on the next page). If the answer is correct, the player gets to pick something from the prize bag. Continue playing until all the questions have been answered.**

1) Lisa's sister died last year and her mother is sad and cries all the time. Circle the best way for Lisa to cope with this:
(a) She should tell her mother jokes to cheer her up
(b) She should pretend to be happy so she does not make her mother feel more upset
(c) She should understand that sadness is a part of grief and crying is normal and healthy

2) Ben's brother died and his parents are so upset that they don't spend much time with him anymore. Circle the best way for Ben to cope with this:
(a) He should ask his therapist to talk with his parents about spending more time with him
(b) He should throw a tantrum until he gets the attention he needs
(c) He should run away from home since his parents don't seem to care about him

3) Tyrel's father died of cancer a few months ago and now he's worried that his mother will get sick and die too. Circle the best way for Tyrel to cope with this:
(a) He should tell himself that his mother will die soon too
(b) He should understand that most people live a long and healthy life
(c) He should stay away from his mother because she may have cancer and he could catch it

4) Ramone has been feeling very angry since his father was killed and he often loses his temper and gets into fights with others. Circle the best way for Ramone to cope with this:
(a) He should take out his anger on his little brother
(b) He should believe he is a bad person because of all the trouble he is getting into
(c) He should try to understand that anger is a normal reaction to grief and he should talk to his therapist about safe ways to express his feelings

5) Mike thinks he is to blame for his father's heart attack, because he was always getting into trouble and his father was often angry at him. Circle the best way for Mike to cope with this:
(a) He should tell himself he made his father die
(b) He should remind himself his father didn't die because of anything he said or did
(c) He should act perfect so people will think he is a good person

6) Mitasha's mother died and she misses her a lot, especially on holidays and special occasions. Circle the best way for Mitasha to cope with this:
(a) She should just forget about her mother
(b) She should avoid celebrating holidays as this will make her feel more sad
(c) She should look at photos of her mother and other keepsakes and this will bring back special memories and help her feel closer to her mother

Coping With Grief Game: Answers

1(c): Even though it's hard for Lisa to see her mother so upset, she should understand that sadness is a part of grief, and crying is a normal, healthy way to let the sadness out.

2(a): Ben's parents are grieving and may not be spending much time with him or giving him the attention he needs. Ben may not feel comfortable talking to his parents on his own about his need for more attention, so his therapist could help by talking to his parents and helping them understand what Ben needs.

3(b): When a parent dies, many children worry about losing their other parent too. Even though it is very sad that Tyrel's father died, he should know that most people live a long and healthy life.

4(c): Anger is a normal reaction to grief. There are many ways to express anger in safe, healthy ways. For example, Ramone could talk to an adult about his anger, or slowly count backward until he feels calm, or visualize a stop sign to stop himself from losing control, or tighten and relax his muscles until his body is relaxed.

5(b): Many children believe they made their loved one die because of something they said or did. But it is important for Mike to know that nothing he said or did caused his father's death.

6(c): When a loved one dies, we miss them, especially on holidays and special occasions. Nobody can take the sadness away, but looking at photos and other keepsakes is a way to bring back special memories and help Mitasha feel closer to her mother.

What I Learned

(Note to therapist: See overview for practitioners for activity preparation and supplies)

Congratulations! You have reached the end of this book. That means you have done a lot of hard work and have learned many things about grief. Answer the questions below to review your thoughts and feelings. For each question you answer, you get to unwrap a layer of the gift. Answer all the questions to get to the gift!

You did many different activities in therapy. Which activities helped you the most?

You learned a lot about grief. What are some things you learned?

Children have different feelings about ending therapy. Some children feel happy to end therapy, some children feel upset about ending therapy. How do you feel about ending therapy?

You have made it through a difficult time. What do you think about yourself now that you have made it through such a difficult time?

You have learned many ways to help yourself through tough times. What are some ways you can help yourself feel better when you are upset in the future?

Giving a Helping Hand

You have learned a lot about dealing with grief and you can give a "helping hand" to others. Trace an outline of your hand in the space below, and on the inside of the hand write a helpful message to other children who are dealing with the death of someone special:

My Feel Better Bag:
My Favorite Feel Better Strategies

Now that you are ending therapy, your *Feel Better Bag* should be filled with ideas to help you feel better. Go through your bag and choose some ideas that have helped you the most. Whenever you are feeling upset, you can use the different ideas from your *Feel Better Bag* to help yourself feel better!

My favorite ideas from my Feel Better Bag:

1._____

2._____

3._____

Looking At This Book

This book is a very special book because all your hard work is inside. Go through your book and see all that you have accomplished. As you go through your book, answer the following questions:

Which activities did you like best?

Which activities were the hardest?

Which activities helped you most?

You will have a chance to show your book to your parent/caregiver when you come here the last time. Go through your book and choose what you want to show them. You can show them your whole book, parts of the book, or none at all. You get to decide what you want to show and what you want to keep private.

You can take this book home if you want to when you come here the last time. Talk with your therapist about where to keep it at home so it is in a safe place. Or, it can be kept here in the office in a locked place, and you can come get it when you are ready. When you look at this book now and when you are older, it will help you remember your special person who died. It will also remind you that you made it through a tough time, and that is something to be really proud of!

Section 9

Interventions to Address Special Issues

Although the interventions in this book have been designed to help grieving children deal with any kind of death, suicide, homicide, and other violent deaths require special intervention. This section includes interventions to help child survivors of suicide and homicide address specific issues. Interventions have also been included here to help children deal with the death of a family member from cancer, as so many children are, unfortunately, faced with this kind of loss. *The Envelope Game* is used to engage children in the session. The *Action Cards* and prizes add to the appeal of the activity and maintain the children's interest in the game. The *Action Cards* also teach and foster coping skills and relaxation techniques. The *Question Cards* can be modified to suit the client's developmental capacities and treatment needs. *The Envelope Game* can be modified to address other special issues, such as AIDS, terrorist attack, natural disasters, etc.

Cancer: Special issues to address when a child is dealing with the death of a family member from cancer include: helping children understand what cancer is, what causes it, and what treatments are available; normalizing feelings; enabling children to understand that they were not responsible for the death; helping children understand that cancer is not contagious.

Suicide: Special issues to address with child survivors of suicide include: defining suicide and helping children understand why someone may have chosen to end their life, alleviating feelings of shame or stigmatization that are typically associated with suicide; enabling children to understand that they were not responsible for the suicide; helping children realize that there are other ways to cope with painful feelings other than suicide. (Although some use the term, *completed suicide*, this book uses the commonly known term of *committed suicide*.)

Homicide: Special issues to address with child survivor-victims of homicide include: validating the victim-survivor role; addressing feelings of rage and fantasies of revenge; enabling children to assign full responsibility for the death to the person who committed the murder; helping children understand issues related to the criminal investigation and legal proceedings; resolving intense feelings of fear and teaching self-soothing strategies.

My Special Person Died From Cancer
(Supplies: Scissors, twelve envelopes, bag filled with small prizes)

Cancer is a disease where sick cells in the body grow out of control and make a lump called a tumor. The tumor makes it hard for the body to work properly. Many people who have cancer get treatment and get better. But some people with cancer get so sick that their body is not able to get well and they die. Cancer is hard to understand and most people feel uncomfortable talking about it. Let's play *The Envelope Game* to learn more about cancer and to make it easier to talk about. To play, cut out the 12 game cards on the next two pages, fold the cards, place each one in a separate envelope, and seal the envelopes. Shuffle the envelopes. Take turns opening an envelope. If the envelope has a Question Card, read it aloud. If the envelope has an Action Card, follow the instructions. If the envelope has a Prize Card, choose a prize from the Prize Bag. Play until all the envelopes have been opened. After you are finished playing *The Envelope Game*, answer the questions below:

What kind of cancer did your special person have?

What kind of medicine or treatment did your special person get and what side effects did you notice from the treatment (i.e. the person lost his/her hair, lost a lot of weight, was tired a lot, etc.)?

After your special person died, how did you feel?

Write or draw about the worst moment for you:

Did you ever feel like the person's death was your fault? How come?

What advice would you give to a child who had a family member die of cancer?

Envelope Game Cards

Question: What is cancer?
Cancer is a disease where sick cells in the body grow and make a lump called a tumor. The tumor makes it hard for the body to work properly. There are many different kinds of cancer. People can die from cancer, but every year doctors are finding new ways of helping people get better from cancer.

Question: What causes cancer, or why do people get cancer?
No one, not even the experts, know what causes cancer. Sometimes children think they made someone get cancer. But people do not get cancer from other people. Doctors and scientists are working very hard to find out more about cancer, so hopefully one day they will know what causes cancer, and how to cure it.

Question: What treatments are there for cancer, and how come they don't work for everybody?
The most common treatments for cancer are surgery (an operation to take out a tumor), radiation (high-energy rays aimed at a tumor to get rid of it), and chemotherapy (strong medicine to get rid of sick cancer cells). Doctors try their best to help make people with cancer better, but some people are so sick that they die. But there are medicines to help people dying from cancer feel better so they do not feel a lot of pain.

Question: How do children feel after someone dies from cancer?
Children have many different feelings after someone dies from cancer. For example: Sad because someone they care about is dead; Scared that something bad will happen; Guilty because they think it is their fault the person got sick and died; Angry because the person died; Worried that they or someone they know will get cancer and die; Relieved because their loved one is not sick and in pain anymore.

Question: Why do some children blame themselves when someone dies from cancer?
There are many reasons why children may think they caused the person to die. They may think they said or did something to cause the person to get cancer and die. They may think they did not do enough to help the person get better. Nothing we think, say, wish or do causes someone to get cancer.

Question: If your friend or family member died from cancer, will you get cancer and die too?
Sometimes children think they will end up dying from cancer just like their parent, sibling, or friend. But you cannot catch cancer, like you can catch a cold. You can't get cancer from someone who has it. Remember that being sick usually does not mean that someone will die. A doctor can cure most people, or they will get better with rest and medicine.

Envelope Game Cards

Action Card:
Hop on one foot for ten seconds, then freeze like a statue for ten seconds

Action Card:
Stomp your feet ten times, then stand still for ten seconds

Action Card:
Take ten slow deep breaths

Action Card:
Jog quickly once around the room, then move around the room in slow motion

Prize!

Prize!

Other Activities about Cancer

Read and talk about the book, *The Rainbow Feelings of Cancer* by C. Martin and C. Martin

Read and talk about the book, *Lost and Found: Remembering a Sister* by E. Yeoman

Read and talk about the book, *The Family Cancer Book* by S. Rugg

Donate a portion of your allowance to a cancer charity in honor of the person who died

My Special Person Died By Suicide

(Supplies: Scissors, twelve envelopes, bag filled with small prizes)

Nobody lives forever. Everybody eventually dies. People die in different ways. For example, some people die from a heart attack, some people die from a car accident, and some people die from suicide. Suicide is when a person chooses to die, and so they do something to make their body stop working. It is awful when someone close to you dies, but when someone dies from suicide, it can be so hard to understand and talk about. Let's play *The Envelope Game* to learn more about suicide and to make it easier to talk about. To play, cut out the 12 game cards on the next two pages, fold the cards, place each one in a separate envelope, and seal the envelopes. Shuffle the envelopes. Take turns opening an envelope. If the envelope has a Question Card, read it aloud. If the envelope has an Action Card, follow the instructions. If the envelope has a Prize Card, choose a prize from the Prize Bag. Play until all the envelopes have been opened. After you are finished playing *The Envelope Game*, answer the questions below:

Why do you think your special person committed suicide?

After your special person committed suicide, how did you feel?

Write or draw about the worst moment for you:

Did you ever feel like the person's death was your fault? How come?

How does it feel when you tell people your loved one died from suicide? Why?

What advice would you give to a child who had a friend or family member die from suicide?

Envelope Game Cards

Question: Why do people choose to die, or commit suicide?
We don't know the exact reason why some people decide to commit suicide. Sometimes it is because they had depression. Depression is a disease that can make people feel very sad and hopeless. They cannot stop the sadness, and they choose to die. Most people with depression get help so they can feel better and want to go on living.

Question: How do people feel after someone dies by suicide?
Children have many different feelings after someone close to them dies by suicide. For example: Sad because someone they care about is dead; Worried that something bad will happen; Guilty because they think it is their fault the person chose to die; Angry because the person chose to die; Embarrassed to tell other people the person died by suicide; Relieved their loved one no longer feels the sadness.

Question: How come it is hard to tell people someone died by suicide?
Suicide is so hard to talk about that sometimes it is easier to say the person died some other way, like from an accident. Sometimes people feel embarrassed to say the person killed themselves because they worry that others will think the person was bad or crazy. But it is important for people to find at least one person they can talk to about what really happened and about how they feel.

Question: Why do some people blame themselves when someone dies by suicide?
There are many reasons why people may think they caused the person's suicide. They may think they said or did something to cause the person to want to die. Or they may blame themselves for not stopping the person from killing themselves. But nothing we think, say, wish or do causes suicide.

Question: Why do some people feel the person who died by suicide did not care about them?
Family and friends of the person who died by suicide may feel like the person did not care about them, because they chose to die instead of wanting to stay alive to be with them. But when someone chooses to die by suicide, they feel so sad and hopeless that they are not thinking right and they cannot think about all the wonderful people in their life. So when someone dies by suicide, it does not mean the person did not love or care about their family and friends.

Question: If someone's friend or family member died by suicide, will they die by suicide too?
Sometimes children think they will end up dying by suicide just like their parent, sibling, or friend. This may be because they feel so sad and wonder if they should end their sadness by choosing to die, in the same way their special person did. They may want to die so they can be with the person who died. If children feel like they want to die, it is important that they talk to an adult about their feelings, so they can get help.

Envelope Game Cards

Action Card:
Hop on one foot for ten seconds, then freeze like a statue for ten seconds

Action Card:
Stomp your feet ten times, then stand still for ten seconds

Action Card:
Take ten slow deep breaths

Action Card:
Jog quickly once around the room, then move around the room in slow motion

Prize!

Prize!

Other Activities about Suicide

Act out the puppet show called "Susie's Suicide" from the book, *Puppet Plays for Grieving Children* by S. Rugg

Read and talk about the book, *Bart Speaks Out: Breaking the Silence on Suicide* by L. Goldman

Read and talk about the book, *But I Didn't Say Goodbye* by Barbara Rubel

My Special Person Was Murdered
(Supplies: Scissors, twelve envelopes, bag filled with small prizes)

Murder is when a person(s) kills another person on purpose. It is awful when someone close to you dies, but when someone you care about is murdered, it can be so hard to accept and to talk about because of the violence involved. Let's play *The Envelope Game* to make it easier to talk about. To play, cut out the 12 game cards on the next two pages, fold the cards, place each one in a separate envelope, and seal the envelopes. Shuffle the envelopes. Take turns opening an envelope. If the envelope has a Question Card, read it aloud. If the envelope has an Action Card, follow the instructions. If the envelope has a Prize Card, choose a prize from the Prize Bag. Play until all the envelopes have been opened. After you are finished playing *The Envelope Game*, answer the questions below:

Who murdered your special person? What do you know about why it happened?

After your special person was killed, how did you feel?

Write or draw about the worst moment for you:

Did you ever feel like the person's death was your fault? How come?

Write a few sentences about what you want to say to the person who killed your special person.

What advice would you give to a child who was dealing with the murder of a close friend or family member?

Envelope Game Cards

Question: What is murder?
Murder is when a person kills another person on purpose. This type of death is called "homicide." It is normal to wonder why people kill people. Often there are no answers to why it happened. People may feel even more confused if the killer was never caught. It can be hard to live with all these unanswered questions. People feel very upset when someone close to them is murdered, but they eventually begin to feel better.

Question: What is a murder investigation and what is a trial?
A person who kills another person commits a crime. A murder investigation is when the police or detectives collect information to find the killer and to learn what happened. If a person is arrested there may be a trial to determine if that person is guilty of the crime, and if s/he should go to jail. If there is a trial, children often hear words they don't understand, like defendant, jury, judge, lawyer, evidence, witness, verdict, and sentence. Children can ask an adult to explain these words to them.

Question: Why is it hard to talk to people about the murder?
It can be hard to tell others about a murder because people often feel uncomfortable hearing about what happened. Sometimes it is easier to say the person died some other way, like from an accident. Sometimes people say hurtful things about the murder, like the person deserved to be killed. It is important for people to find someone to talk to about what really happened and about how they feel about the murder.

Question: Why do some people blame themselves when someone they care about is murdered?
It is normal for people to feel like they could have stopped the person from getting killed. They might think if they stopped the person from going out, they wouldn't have gotten killed. Or if they had been there, they could have stopped it from happening. Or they might think their thoughts caused it, like if they thought, "I wish you were dead." But words or thoughts don't cause someone to die. When someone dies because of violence, the only person to blame is the one who did the violent act.

Question: Why do people often feel angry when someone they care about is murdered?
Anger is a common feeling to have when someone is murdered. People may feel angry at the murderer for killing the person, at God for letting this happen, at the person who was killed for not getting away, or at themselves for not stopping it. They may want to get even with or even hurt the murderer. It is normal and okay to feel angry, but it is important to let out anger in safe ways.

Question: Why do children often feel afraid when someone they care about is murdered?
When a family member or friend is murdered, children often feel afraid. They may have scary thoughts or bad dreams about it. They may worry that other bad things will happen. They may feel afraid to be alone or to go certain places. There are things children can do to feel safer, like thinking of a safe place, sleeping with a stuffed animal, or staying close to an adult they trust.

Envelope Game Cards

Action Card:
Hop on one foot for ten seconds, then freeze like a statue for ten seconds

Action Card:
Stomp your feet ten times, then stand still for ten seconds

Action Card:
Take ten slow deep breaths

Action Card:
Jog quickly once around the room, then move around the room in slow motion

Prize!

Prize!

Other Activities You Might Find Helpful
if Someone in Your Family Was Murdered

Read and talk about the book, *After a Murder* by The Dougy Center

Read and talk about the book, *Jenny is Scared: When Sad Things Happen in the World* by C. Shuman

Write a letter to the judge explaining how your loved one's murder has affected you.

Pretend that you are the judge in charge of deciding what happens to the person who killed your family member or friend. Make up a skit about it.

Section 10

Interventions for Group Sessions

Bereaved children can benefit greatly from participating in group therapy. The group setting provides a developmentally appropriate environment in which children can share their thoughts and feelings about the death. Group therapy offers the following advantages:

- Allows assessment of child's functioning: The group becomes a microcosm of society so it allows the therapist to gain insight into the children's presentation in their everyday lives.
- Promotes universality: Allows children to see that they are not the only ones grieving This counters elements of secrecy, isolation, and the sense of "being different"
- Facilitates vicarious learning: Children observe the expressions of fellow group members and learn from others.
- Encourages greater risk-taking and catharsis: Children who are initially cautious to explore and express certain issues may open up as they see other peers engage in activities.
- Enhances interpersonal skills: Children have the opportunity to interact with peers and master new behaviors.

Ethical and Legal Considerations

There are a number of ethical and legal considerations that practitioners must adhere to when facilitating groups for bereaved children:
- The practitioner must have proper training and supervision in group therapy with bereaved children.
- Group leaders should be covered by Professional Liability Insurance.
- Written consent for the child's participation in group must be obtained from all legal custodians.
- In the event that a child discloses abuse during group, proper channels for reporting must be followed.
- Group leaders should adhere to standards of practice regarding record-keeping.
- A clinical file should be kept on each group member, and a copy of each activity placed in the file.
- Participant contract ensuring group confidentiality should be secured at the start of the first session.

Group Leadership

Effective group leadership is essential to creating a safe and caring therapeutic environment. If the group is run by co-leaders, they must model respect for one another, agree on roles and the structure and content of the group, and have compatible beliefs about how to work with bereaved children. A skilled clinical supervisor can assist co-leaders in developing a good working relationship.

Group Composition

Consideration must be given to the group composition. In terms of size, children's groups should be kept fairly small in order to best respond to the emotional and behavioral needs of the children. The group can be mixed gender with an appropriate balance of girls and boys. The age range of the members should generally not exceed twelve months. Some children are not group-appropriate. Ginott (1961) suggested the following contraindications: (1) Extremely aggressive children; (2) Sexually acting-out children; (3) Children with serious psychiatric disturbances; and (4) Siblings who exhibit intense rivalry. Decisions regarding group composition must be based on maximizing the children's sense of safety and positive clinical experience.

Assessment and Screening

Each child should be assessed individually to determine his or her clinical needs and if the group is the most appropriate treatment modality. The assessment interventions in Section Four can be used as part of this assessment, along with the Parent Questionnaire in Section Three. If the child participated in a group before, the group leader should determine whether the child managed well in that situation.

Group Structure and Content

The length and number of sessions can vary, but generally groups for younger children should be shorter, given their limited attention span, i.e. 45-60 minutes, and groups for school-aged and adolescent clients 60-90 minutes. The number of sessions will depend on the group curriculum.

Each session should adhere to a similar structure, so the group members know what to expect. It can be helpful to begin each session with a grief-focused opening ritual. One idea is an African ritual called a libation, in which the names of deceased family and friends get called out, and as the names are called, water is poured into a plant. This ritual develops a sense of safety for the group talking about death, and honors those who have died. A check-in should also be included at the beginning of each group, to assess current functioning and facilitate self-expression. For example, each child can point to a feeling face on a chart to indicate how s/he is feeling. A quick ice-breaker game can then be played. There are many excellent resources containing group ice-breakers, such as *Games for Group* (Cavert, 1999) and *Quicksilver* (Rohnke and Butler, 1995). Next, the group members can complete the grief-specific treatment activities planned for the session. (The leader should be prepared to divert from the planned activity if needed.) While the interventions in this section have been designed specifically for use in group counseling, many interventions from this book can be modified for the group format. (A *Sample Group Curriculum* has been included, to give an idea of group structure and content.) A fun closing activity can be initiated to help end the session on a lighter note.

Sample Group Curriculum

The following are suggested interventions for a ten-week group for bereaved children, ages 7-12. Each group member should be assessed and screened prior to group, and if needed, provided with individual and/or family therapy, as an adjunct to group counseling. In addition to the interventions listed below, each session should begin with an icebreaker, and end with a fun and energetic closing activity. Each group member should be given a scrapbook in the first session, and all their activities should be placed in this book. A session with the child and his or her caregiver should be scheduled at the end to provide feedback and treatment recommendations.

Session # 1: Getting Acquainted
Goals: (1) Establish group rapport and cohesion (2) Define the purpose of the group and rules
Interventions: (1) Welcome Letter (2) Decorate scrapbook cover (3) About Me (4) Balloon Bounce

Session #2: Understanding Death
Goals: (1) Verbalize an understanding of death (2) Increase comfort level talking about death
Interventions: (1) About Death Puzzle (2) What Causes Death (3) Scavenger Hunt

Session #3: Identifying & Expressing Feelings Associated with Grief
Goals: (1) Normalize and identify feelings associated with grief
Interventions: (1) Ali and Her Mixed-Up Feeling Jar (2) Go Fish (Lowenstein, 2002, p.35)

Session #4: Sharing Stories
Goals: (1) Share circumstances of the death (2) Express thoughts and feelings regarding death
Interventions: (1) My Special Person's Death (2) Group Card Game

Session #5: Identifying and Expressing Sadness
Goals: (1) Identify and express sad feelings associated with the death
Interventions: (1) Feeling Sad (2) Read and process the book, *Tear Soup* (Schwiebert and Deklyen)

Session #6: Identifying and Expressing Anger
Goals: (1) Identify and express angry feelings associated with the death (2) Identify safe ways to express anger
Interventions: (1) Feeling Angry (2) Road Rage (Lowenstein, 2002, p. 64)

Session #7: Preserving Memories of the Deceased
Goals: (1) Discuss the importance of memories (2) Recall and share memories of the deceased (3) Understand that memories can live on forever
Interventions: (1) My Special Person (2) What I Liked and Didn't Like (3) Penny for Your Thoughts

Session #8: Saying Goodbye to the Deceased
Goals: (1) Communicate unfinished business to the person who died (2) Say goodbye to the person who died (3) Provide a comforting memorial
Interventions: (1) Saying Goodbye (2) Handkerchief (McKissock, 2004, p. 190)

Session #9: Coping with Grief
Goals: (1) Implement adaptive coping strategies
Interventions: (1) Coping with Grief Attacks (2) Feel Good Messages

Session #10: Termination
Goals: (1) Review gains in therapy (2) Celebrate accomplishments made in therapy (3) Provide positive termination experience (4) Say goodbye to each other
Interventions: (1) Giving a Helping Hand (2) Pizza Party

Therapeutic Responses

Facilitating a group for bereaved children requires clinical skill. One important skill is to provide appropriate therapeutic responses to group members. Below are some examples:

<u>Reflecting interaction</u>: *"Johnny and Mike, you don't want to sit beside each other because you are still mad about what happened last session."*
<u>Reflecting content</u>: *"Sounds like everyone in the group misses the person who died."*
<u>Reflecting feelings</u>: *"Johnny, you feel guilty for not visiting your mom when she was in the hospital."*
<u>Tracking behavior</u>: *"Johnny, you are feeling angry so you are stomping your feet."*
<u>Limit setting</u>: *"Johnny, you're angry at Mike for calling you stupid, but it is not okay to hit Mike. Use your words to let Mike know you feel angry."*
<u>Enlarging the meaning</u>: *"Johnny, you feel like your mom's death was your fault. Children often feel that way. Who else in the group feels like they are to blame?"*

Common Group Therapy Mistakes

Group therapy can be a powerful treatment modality for bereaved children. However, group facilitators can hinder the group process by making the following mistakes:

- Inadequately screening members for group appropriateness and readiness.
- Facilitating mini sessions in group rather than utilizing the group.
- Focusing on content more than process.
- Not allowing the children to speak and work out issues together.

Under the right circumstances, group therapy can be tremendously therapeutic for bereaved children. Being with other children who have suffered a similar loss has the greatest power to normalize a child's experience.

Interventions

Balloon Bounce: It is helpful to begin a first group session with an icebreaker. The *Balloon Bounce* activity helps group members get to know one another, and it facilitates communication and group cohesion. To prepare the activity, write a *Getting Acquainted* question onto each balloon. (Use a black permanent marker to write the questions onto the balloons to avoid smudging.) Examples of questions include:

What do you like to do for fun?
What's your favorite food?
What's a food you really hate?
What's your favorite movie?
What's your favorite game?
What makes you feel excited?
What's something that really bugs you?
When was the best day of your life?

The questions can be modified to suit the age and needs of the group. Suggested processing questions include: What new information did you learn about the members of the group? What did you discover about the things you have in common with other group members? How are you different from the others in the group? What is important about getting to know the others in the group?

Scavenger Hunt: This intervention promotes communication regarding death, catharsis of feelings, and problem-solving. It encourages creative thinking and open dialogue among group members. Copy the list of *Scavenger Hunt* items so each group has their own. A group leader should be assigned to each sub-group to assist with reading and writing and to facilitate appropriate group interaction.

Group Card Game: This therapeutic game helps the group explore a number of treatment issues, including: Understanding death; Expressing feelings related to the death; Exploring feelings of guilt, sadness, and anger; Accepting the finality of the death. The active component of the game (the *Action Cards*) helps to channel the children's energy into positive outlets. To prepare the game, copy each *Question Card* and *Action Card* onto separate index cards or photocopy the *Card Sheets* onto colored card stock and cut out each card. (The questions can be adapted depending on the ages of the children and treatment needs of the group.) Place the *Question Cards* and *Action Cards* in two separate piles in the middle of the group. The *Guide* can be placed beside the question cards for easy reference during the game. Process the game at the end by asking the members what they learned about grief.

Pizza Party: This activity can be used in a final group session as a creative way to affirm therapeutic gains, as well as provide the opportunity to discuss the children's feelings about termination. The celebratory atmosphere that is created in the session facilitates a positive termination experience for the children. To prepare the activity, make a copy of the *Pizza Party* worksheet for each group member. Photocopy the puzzle onto colored card stock and cut along the dotted lines to make six cardboard pizza slices. Place the six cardboard pizza slices in a small bag. Obtain permission from caregivers to offer pizza to the children.

Balloon Bounce: A Group Ice-Breaker Game
(Supplies: One balloon per group member and leader, black permanent marker)

This game will help us get to know one another. It is called *Balloon Bounce*. Each group member will get a balloon. The balloons have questions written on them to help us get to know one another. At the count of three, we will throw the balloons in the air and try to keep them in the air without them touching the ground. When I yell, "Stop!" everyone will let the balloons fall to the ground. One group member will be chosen to pick up a balloon and answer the question written on it. Everyone will get a chance. Once everyone has answered the question, we will throw the balloons back into the air and play another round. The game will continue until we have answered all the questions on the balloons.

Scavenger Hunt

(Supplies: Paper, markers)

You will be divided into two teams. Each team will get a list of items to collect. You will have 15 minutes to collect as many items on the list that you can. The team that collects the most items from the list wins.

Scavenger Hunt Items

Picture of a grieving child

4 feelings children may have when someone close to them dies

Something blue

2 people with the same shoe size

Something living

3 safe ways to express anger

Outline of a hand

Words of advice to help children who feel the death was their fault

Something that can help grieving children

A group of children holding hands and singing a song

The Group Card Game
(Supplies: Deck of playing cards, cookies)

It can be hard to talk about the death of someone close, so let's play a card game to make it easier. To play, take turns picking the top card from the stack of cards. If you get a card with an even number (2,4,6,8,10) pick a question card and answer the question. If you do not feel you can answer the question, you can ask the group for help. If you get a card with an odd number (3,5,7,9) pick an action card and follow the instructions. If you pick an ace, skip a turn. If you pick a jack, do 10 jumping jacks. If you pick a queen or king, you get a cookie. At the end of the game, everyone who played gets a cookie.

Guide

Even cards = Question card

Odd cards = Action card

Ace = Skip turn

Jack = Do 10 jumping jacks

Queen, King = Get cookie

Question Cards:
The Group Card Game

(1) What is grief?	**(2) True or False: All living things eventually die**	**(3) Name 3 things that can cause people to die**
(4) Name 3 feelings children may have when someone close to them dies	**(5) Is death contagious?**	**(6) Why do children sometimes hide their sad feelings?**
(7) True or False: It is normal to have a hard time believing a person is really dead	**(8) True or False: People sometimes blame themselves for the death**	**(9) True or False: A dead body cannot move, breathe, or feel anything**
(10) True or False: Most people don't want to talk about death	**(11) What is a funeral?**	**(12) What is a cemetery?**
(13) What is a coffin?	**(14) What is cremation?**	**(15) What is a memory?**
(16) If someone in your family dies, does that mean you will die soon too?	**(17) True or False: Many people find it hard to feel sad when someone dies because they are in shock**	**(18) True or False: Children shouldn't cry because it makes them look like a cry baby**
(19) Do grieving children ever worry they are going crazy?	**(20) True or False: A child who misbehaved a lot is to blame for the death**	**(21) True or False: If a child tries hard enough s/he can bring the dead person back alive**
(22) What is a safe way to handle angry feelings?	**(23) What can children do to feel better when they are upset?**	**(24) True or False: When someone close to you dies you will feel sad forever**

Answers:
The Group Card Game

1) What is grief? Grief refers to the feelings, thoughts and reactions people have when someone dies.

2) True or False: All living things eventually die. True. Death is natural and everything that lives eventually dies. Plants die. Animals die. People die.

3) Name three things that can cause people to die. Many things can cause people to die, like they get very sick, someone else hurts them, they get into a bad accident, they kill themselves, or they die from old age.

4) Name three feelings children may have when someone close to them dies. Children may experience many different feelings when someone dies, such as, sad, angry, guilty, worried, confused, embarrassed, and relieved.

5) Is death contagious? Death is not contagious. Just because someone we know dies, it does not mean that we will die soon too. You can't catch death like you can catch a cold. Most people live a long time.

6) Why do children sometimes hide their feelings? Children may hide their feelings because they don't want others to know how they feel. But it is important for children to find at least one person they can talk to about their true feelings.

7) True or False: It is normal to have a hard time believing a person is really dead. True. People may have a hard time believing a person is really dead because it is hard to accept a person is gone forever.

8) True or False: People sometimes blame themselves for the death. True. People may feel like the death was their fault. They may think their thoughts, words or wishes made the person die. But our thoughts, words, or wishes cannot make someone die.

9) True or False: A dead body cannot move, breathe, or feel anything. True. A dead body cannot move, breathe, or feel anything.

10) True or False: Most people don't want to talk about death. True. It is hard to talk about death. But the more you talk about it, the easier it gets.

11) What is a funeral? A funeral is when family and friends come together to say goodbye to the person who died and to remember the good things about the dead person.

12) What is a cemetery? A cemetery is a place where dead people are buried.

13) What is a coffin? A coffin is a wooden or steel box that holds the body of the person who died.

14) What is cremation? Cremation is when a dead body is burned in very high heat and turned into ashes. Being cremated may seem weird, scary or gross, but the person who died cannot feel anything. It does not hurt because the dead person cannot feel any pain.

15) What is a memory? A memory is something you remember about the person who died or something you did with them. It is important to write or draw some memories of the person who died so you do not forget them.

16) If someone in your family dies, does that mean you will die soon too? No. Most people live a long time and die when they are old.

17) True or False: Many people find it hard to feel sad when someone dies because they are in shock. True. Some people are in shock when someone dies and they feel numb, which means they feel nothing at all. It can take time for some people to be ready to feel the pain and sadness of grief.

18) True or False: Children shouldn't cry because it makes them look like a cry baby. False. Crying is a normal way to let out sad feelings.

19) Do grieving children ever worry they are going crazy? Yes. Grieving children may have many strong feelings and reactions when someone dies, so they may think they are going crazy. But these feelings and reactions do not make a person crazy—they are a normal part of grief.

20) True or False: A child who misbehaved a lot is to blame for the death. False. Death does not happen because of bad behavior or because of anything a child did.

21) True or False: If a child tries hard enough s/he can bring the dead person back alive. False. Once someone is dead they stay dead, and there is nothing a child can do to bring the person back alive.

22) What is a safe way to handle angry feelings? Safe anger means expressing anger in a way that does not hurt yourself or anybody else. Some safe ways to express anger are: talking to an adult, writing or drawing about feelings, walking away, helping your body to feel calm and relaxed.

23) What can children do to feel better when they are upset? Some ways children can help themselves feel better when they are upset are drawing or writing about their feelings, or talking to someone.

24) True or False: When someone close to you dies you will feel sad forever. False. When someone close to you dies, sad feelings come and go. There will be times when you feel sad, and times when you feel happy. There are things you can do to help yourself feel better when you have sad times.

Action Cards:
The Group Card Game

Hop to the other end of the room and back on one foot	Spin your body around five times then try to touch your nose with your thumb	Switch seats with someone in the group
Jump up and down ten times	Shake hands with someone in the group	Give someone in the group a high-five
Do ten jumping jacks	Switch seats with the person sitting to your left	Give a high-five to the person sitting to your left
Give a high-five to the person sitting to your right	Switch seats with the person sitting to your right	Stomp your feet ten times
Touch your toes	Shake hands with the person sitting to your left	Stand on your toes for five seconds
Take five slow deep breaths	Shake hands with the person sitting to your right	Give yourself a hug

Pizza Party

(Supplies: Small bag filled with the cardboard pizza slices, dice, party hats, transparent tape, pizza)

Today we are going to honor and celebrate the progress you made in this group by playing a party game. To do that, each of you will complete a worksheet, and then we are going to play a game called *Pizza Party*. At the end of the game, we get a special treat!

(Distribute a party hat for each group member to wear, and a *Pizza Party* worksheet for each group member to complete. Once the worksheets have been completed, group members sit in a circle with their completed worksheets in front of them. The bag filled with the six puzzle pieces is placed in the middle of the circle.)

We will now play *The Pizza Party Game*. To play, we will take turns rolling the dice and answering the question on the worksheet that matches the number on the dice. For example, when a player rolls 2, that player shares his or her answer for question number 2 on the worksheet ("The group activity that helped me the most"). All players then share their answer for question 2. The player who rolled the dice then draws a cardboard pizza slice from the bag. Each cardboard pizza slice represents an item for a pizza. All six cardboard pizza slices must be earned in order to complete the pizza puzzle. The game is played until all six numbers of the dice have been rolled and each of the six questions on the worksheet has been answered. If during the game, a player rolls a number that has already been used, the player rolls again until a new number comes up. When all the questions have been answered and the six cardboard pizza slices have been earned, the group will put the cardboard pizza puzzle together. The group is then awarded a special treat: pizza!

Worksheet
Pizza Party

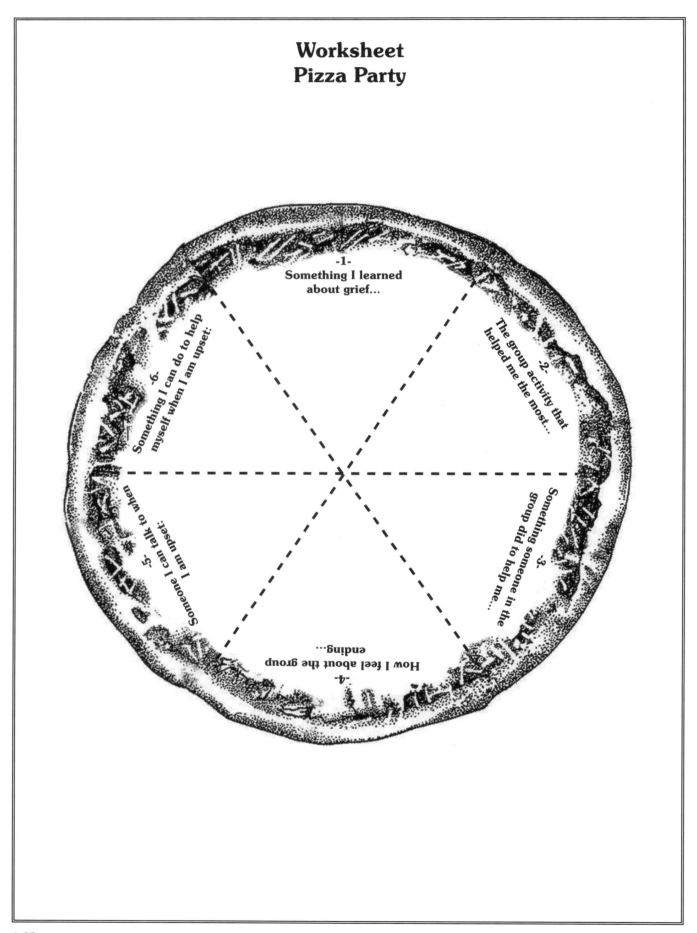

-1-
Something I learned
about grief...

-2-
The group activity that
helped me the most...

-3-
Something someone in the
group did to help me....

-4-
How I feel about the group
ending...

-5-
Someone I can talk to when
I am upset:

-6-
Something I can do to help
myself when I am upset:

Pizza Party Puzzle

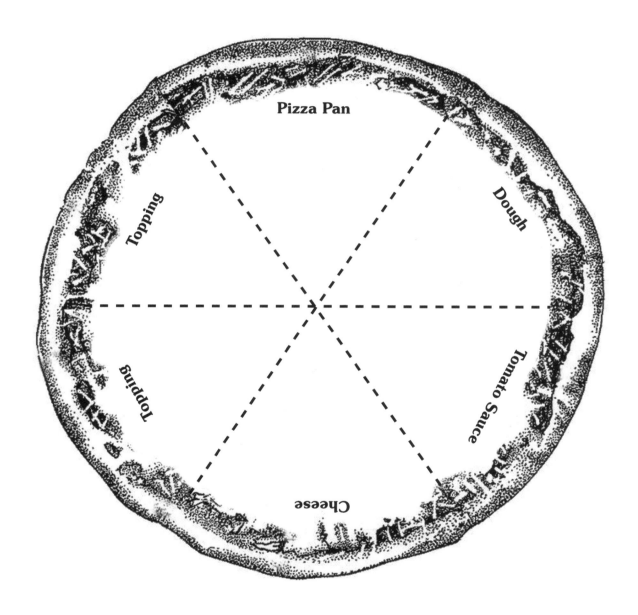

Section 11

Interventions for Family Sessions

Involving families in the treatment of bereaved children is highly beneficial to both the child and the family. According to Walsh and McGoldrick (1991), and Cohen, et al. (2001), treatment goals with bereaved families include:

- Enabling each family member to openly grieve in a way that is developmentally appropriate and culturally sensitive
- Facilitating open communication about the death and other issues
- Helping the caregiver appropriately explain the death to the children
- Helping the caregiver to create a safe and consistent environment
- Facilitating mourning rituals as a means of healing
- Helping the family to reorganize itself after the loss
- Enabling the family to become reinvested in the "new" family
- Providing hope for healing

Rationale for Use of Play in Family Therapy

Play-based interventions can be incorporated into family sessions. Gil (1994) outlines the following benefits for using play in family therapy:

- Provides a comfortable medium for children
- Engages family members in a common, pleasurable task
- Facilitates a broad scope of diagnostic information
- Unlocks a deeper level of communication
- Exposes underlying thoughts and feelings
- Encourages family relatedness

This section includes a number of play-based family interventions, namely, art, games and storytelling.

Role of the Family Therapist

The role of the family therapist is to:

- Engage all family members
- Create a safe place for mourning
- Introduce and lead the activities
- Assess family dynamics
- Model new patterns and skills
- Offer interpretations that will facilitate healthy family functioning
- Discuss how family play activities can be integrated into home settings

The practitioner can meet with the parent(s) ahead of time to explain the importance of the family's involvement in the therapy, and to pre-empt the family's resistance to engaging in the play activities by conveying the expectation that the family will benefit from this technique.

Interventions

Family Gift: It is helpful to assess the family dynamics that contribute to the child's functioning and adjustment. Evaluating children within the context of their family can provide useful clinical information that assists in the development of treatment goals. Infants and toddlers should be included in the session, even though they are too young to directly participate in the activity. The practitioner uses *The Family Gift* technique to assess the following family dynamics: a) Who makes the decisions? b) How well can the parent organize without over-controlling? c) Can the parent encourage the child's ideas rather than imposing their own? d) Which member's suggestions were utilized and which were ignored? e) Were they able to negotiate and reach consensus? d) Who made friendly gestures and who made hostile gestures? f) Did the interaction take on a structure, or was it chaotic? g) What was the level of affect? h) Was the parent able to set appropriate limits and offer praise and affection? i) If there is more than one child, can the parent appropriately attend to the needs of each child? j) Did any dysfunctional patterns emerge, i.e. parentification, triangulation, disengagement, scapegoating, overfunctioning? k) Who engaged in the activity and enjoyed the play?

The Family Card Game: This is a useful diagnostic and treatment tool. It enables the family to communicate more openly, have a shared understanding of the death, strengthens support between parent and child, and facilitates healthy coping. To prepare the game, copy each question from the list provided onto separate index cards, or photocopy the question card sheet onto colored card stock and cut out each question. (The questions can be adapted depending on the ages of the children and the treatment needs of the family.) At the end of the game, process the activity by asking the family what they learned about one another and what they learned about grief.

Family Changes: After the death of a family member, particularly the death of a parent, an important goal of family intervention is to identify new roles within the family and facilitate healthy restructuring. This activity uses a story and puppet reenactment as a way for the family to explore their grief, focus on changes in roles and structure within the family, and negotiate new roles to aid in family readjustment. The story can be modified as needed.

Family Memory Book: Commemorating the deceased is one of the goals of grief therapy. *The Family Memory Book,* an activity that facilitates this goal, can be done with a child in individual therapy, but is best done as a family activity, as it provides a way for families to talk about the deceased with one another. As an added activity, the family can take photos of things at home that remind them of the deceased, and paste these photos with captions into *The Memory Book*.

Candle-Lighting Ceremony: This grieving ritual facilitates memory work and emotional release. It can be very healing for the family. It is important to debrief with the family after the ritual and provide a supportive presence.

Ways to Honor and Remember Our Loved One: It is important to help the family recognize the importance of ongoing grief rituals and to provide them with ways they can commemorate the deceased. They can choose from the list provided in this activity, and they can add their own ideas.

Postcards: Children often have difficulty expressing their feelings and needs to their parents. This intervention helps to open communication between parents and children about difficult issues. It gives children the words to express their thoughts and needs, and it guides parents to respond appropriately. It is suggested that the practitioner meet with the parents prior to involving the child in the session, to review the content of the *Postcards*, and prepare them to respond in a sensitive manner.

Nightly Snuggle: Children need comfort and attention from their parents, yet many parents have difficulty providing their children with these basic needs, particularly grieving parents who may be preoccupied with their own distress. This intervention helps parents attend to their children's need for physical affection and quality time. If the relationship between a parent and child is strained, the parent will need additional guidance from the practitioner on how to engage the child.

Our Family Can Shine: An essential goal in grief therapy is to instill hope for the family's capacity to heal. It is important for the family to see how far they have come in their grief journey and to recognize their individual and collective strength to survive and to be happy again.

Family Gift
(Supplies: Gift bag, craft supplies such as markers, tape, cardboard, popsicle sticks, pipe cleaners etc.)

This activity is called *The Family Gift*. Create a gift for your family using any of the supplies provided. It should be a gift that everyone in the family wants. It can only be one gift, and you must all agree what the gift should be, and how it might be used in your family. Once you have created your gift, place it in the gift bag. You have 30 minutes to decide and create your gift.

When you are done (or the 30 minutes is up) answer the questions below:

Describe your gift

Tell how you each felt as you were creating your gift

Who made the decisions? For example, who decided what the gift should be?

Were two or more people in your family able to cooperate and work well together?

Did anyone cause any difficulties or disagreements, and if so, how was this handled?

Is there anything about the way you did the activity that reminds you of how things work in your family at home?

How can the gift help your family? What else can help your family?

The Family Card Game
(Supplies: Deck of cards, cookies)

This game will help your family talk together about your special person's death. To play, take turns picking the top card from the deck of cards. If you get a card with an even number, pick a card from the *Question Card* pile and answer the question. If you get a card with an odd number, pick a card from the *Question Card* pile and ask someone in your family to answer the question. The *Question Cards* will help you talk about how things are in your family, your feelings about your special person's death, ways you can cope with your feelings, and memories of the person who died. If you do not feel you can answer the question, you can ask your family for help. If you pick an ace, ask someone in your family for a hug. If you pick a jack, do 10 jumping jacks. If you pick a queen or king, you get a cookie. At the end of the game, everyone who played gets a cookie.

Guide

Even cards = You answer

Odd cards = You choose a family member to answer

Ace = Ask for a hug

Jack = Do 10 jumping jacks

Queen, King = Get cookie

Question Cards:
The Family Card Game

Tell three feelings you have had since the person died	Tell about a worry you have had since the person died	In what ways has your family changed since the person died?
Did you ever feel like you caused the person to die?	What's a question you have had since the person died?	What would you say to someone who thought they should hide their sad feelings?
Tell something that is different at home since the person died	Can you wish someone dead and then they will die?	What is something you would like to change about your family?
Share a favorite memory of the person who died	Tell one happy and one sad memory about the person who died	What is something you are looking forward to doing together as a family
What would you like to say to the person who died?	What is something you can do that would be helpful for your whole family?	Tell about a new chore, job, or role you have in your family since the death and how you feel about it
What advice would you give a child who felt he was not getting enough attention?	What three words best describe the person who died?	What is something your family can do on the anniversary of the person's death?
What do you believe happens to people after they die?	Tell about a grieving ritual or custom your family followed when the person died	Once a person is dead, can they come back alive?
What is a healthy way to express angry feelings?	Tell about a time someone in your family did something nice for you	What advice would you give to someone who worried others in their family were going to die soon too?
What helps you feel better when you are upset?	Tell about a holiday spent with the person who died	What is something you learned from the person who died?
Describe what the person who died looked like	What has helped you the most since the person died?	What do you appreciate most about your family?

Family Changes
(Supplies: Materials to make puppets)

When a family member dies, each person reacts to the death in his or her own way. The death of a family member can also bring many changes at home-- changes in how each person in your family feels, and changes in how things work in your family. This activity will help your family talk about how each of you has reacted to the death, and about the different changes at home. To begin, make five puppets to represent the characters in the story on the next page, i.e. make a mother, father, and three children. Then use the puppets to act out the story on the next page as it is read aloud (decide which puppets each of you will use to act out the story).

After the story is read aloud, answer the questions below:

How did each person in the family feel and react to the death? How is this similar or different to how each of you felt/reacted after the death?

What changed in the family after the death? What changed in your family after the death, i.e. what new roles or responsibilities do you have now? How do you feel about these changes?

What do you think would help make things better in your family now?

Family Changes

This is a story about the Smith family. They were a pretty typical family until something terrible happened. Molly Smith, their much loved <u>wife and mother</u>, died. Everyone felt very sad. They each reacted in their own way. <u>Dad</u> got busy at work so he didn't have to think about how much he missed his wife. But he also felt scared—scared about how to raise his children all on his own. <u>Kate, the eldest child</u>, felt so sad and depressed. She had a hard time concentrating at school and her grades dropped. <u>Brian, the middle child</u>, thought his mom's death was his fault—that God took his mom away to punish him for being bad. He started to throw tantrums over the smallest things, and get into fights with other kids at school. <u>The youngest child, Jake,</u> didn't believe his mom was really dead. He thought if he was really good, maybe his mom would surprise him and come back on his birthday.

There were lots of changes at home. Dad suddenly found himself having to be both father and mother to his children. It was hard to juggle it all—working long hours at his very busy job, running the household, driving his children to after-school activities. He felt so overwhelmed! And there were things he was not used to having to do, like getting groceries and cooking family meals. His wife used to do those things. He asked his eldest daughter to help with the cooking and to take care of her brothers after school. This made her angry because it interfered with the time she got to hang out with her friends. And besides, she didn't think it was fair that she had to do all this stuff. Brian was upset too. He didn't like how his sister had become so mean and bossy since their mom died. And he felt angry that he had to quit the baseball team because there was no one to drive him to practice. Jake felt angry too--angry that his mom wasn't around to tuck him into bed at night, and angry at his sister for calling him a cry-baby.

The family went for help. They talked about their feelings with each other. They came up with a plan for everyone to pitch in at home. They shared memories of the good times spent with their mom. After a while, things got better. They all still missed mom, but their special memories of her made them feel happy once again.

Family Memory Book
(Supplies: Paper, coloring supplies, stapler)

Your family shared many times with your special person before he or she died. It is important to capture these memories so you don't forget them. Draw or write about some favorite memories of the person who died, then compile them in a *Family Memory Book*. Decide together as a family on a title for the book, then work together to decorate the cover of the *Memory Book*. Talk about your memories, and decide on a family ritual for looking at the book. For example, each year on the anniversary of the death date.

Candle-Lighting Ceremony
(Supplies: Candles, foil, matches, remembrance music, CD player)

One way to honor your special person's memory is to have a candle-lighting ceremony. You may wish to invite other family members to this ceremony. You can follow the script below, or write your own:

(Gather in a circle. Place a candle for each participant on a sheet of foil in the middle of the circle. Dim the lights.)

We gather here today to remember someone who was very special. Let's begin by listening to a piece of music. (Play remembrance music.)

We are each going to take turns lighting a candle in memory of (name of the person who died). As you light your candle, think about a memory you have of (name of the person who died). (Each participant lights a candle. Read the poem below.)

We Remember Them (Gates of Prayer, Reform Judaism Prayer Book)
In the rising of the sun and in its going down, We remember them
In the blowing of the wind and in the chill of winter, We remember them
In the opening of the buds and in the warmth of summer, We remember them
In the rustling of leaves and the beauty of autumn, We remember them
In the beginning of the year and when it ends, We remember them
When we are weary and in need of strength, We remember them
When we are lost and sick of heart, We remember them
When we have joys we yearn to share, We remember them
So long as we live, they too shall live, For they are now a part of us, as
We remember them

I now invite each of you to share your memory. (Take turns sharing a memory of your special person who died. End by playing another piece of music or reading something that would be meaningful to the person who died.)

As we blow out the candles, let us remember that even though our loved one has died, their memory will live on forever. (Blow out the candles.) *Let us end by joining hands and having a moment of silence.*

Ways to Honor and Remember Our Loved One

There are many ways your family can honor and remember the person who died. Below is a list of ideas. Every once in a while, choose something from the list for your family to do together—it will help keep the memory of your special person alive!

Look at family photo albums

Plant a flower or tree in memory of your special person who died

Make pillows out of your special person's shirts or sweaters

Have a party on your special person's birthday to celebrate his or her life

Do something your special person enjoyed in his or her honor

Cook your special person's favorite foods and have a feast in his or her honor

Go on a memory photo outing. Photograph your special person's favorite places and put them in an album. Add captions to the photos

Donate a gift, money, or flowers in the person's name

Visit the cemetery where the person is buried

Other ideas:

Postcards
(Supplies: Postcards, colored markers)

Sometimes it can be hard for children to talk to their parents about their feelings or needs. Writing it down can make it easier. Below are some examples of feelings and needs children may have. Copy each one onto a postcard, and decorate them (the parent can do the writing and the child can do the decorating.) Take the postcards home and decide together where to keep them so they can be used when needed.

Dear mom/dad,
I feel upset and need to talk to you.
Love,
_____

PS: Please write back.

Dear mom/dad,
I feel ignored or left out and need more attention from you.
Love,
_____

PS: Please write back.

Dear mom/dad,
Someone is hurting me but I'm afraid to tell you about it.
Love,
_____

PS: Please write back.

Dear mom/dad,
I think (name of person who died) death was my fault. Is that true?
Love,
_____

PS: Please write back.

Dear mom/dad,
I really miss (name of person who died) and feel sad, but I worry if I cry, or talk about (name of person who died) it will make you more sad. What should I do?
Love,
_____

PS: Please write back.

Postcards Tip Sheet

(For parents) Take this tip-sheet home in case you need guidance on how to respond to your child.

Child: I feel upset and need to talk to you.
Parent response: I am here to listen. You can tell me anything.

Child: I feel ignored or left out and need more attention from you.
Parent response: Let's plan some special time together, just you and I.

Child: Someone is hurting me but I'm afraid to tell you about it.
Parent response: Please tell me so I can help make the hurting stop. You can tell me anything and I won't be mad at you.

Child: I think the death was my fault. Is that true?
Parent response: Nothing you did, said, thought, or felt made (name of person who died) die.

Child: I really miss (name of person who died) and feel sad, but I worry if I cry, or talk about (name of person who died) it will make you more sad. What should I do?
Parent response: It's okay for you to cry—crying is a good way for you to let out your sad feelings. And it is important for us to talk about (name of person who died) so we don't forget him/her. I feel sad sometimes, but I will be okay.

Nightly Snuggle

Dear parents,
All children need comfort. But when someone close to them dies, children need extra comfort. The nightly snuggle is a ritual you can do with your child each night at bedtime. Snuggle with your child, and ask him or her about his or her day, i.e. was your day <u>terrible</u>, <u>okay</u>, or <u>great</u> and what happened to make it terrible, okay, or great? If your child reports a terrible day, and you are not sure how to respond, here are some suggestions:

<u>Repeat</u>: You feel upset because…

<u>Normalize</u>: It's normal and okay to feel upset about…

<u>Explore</u>: Tell me more about your sad feelings

<u>Praise</u>: I'm glad you can talk to me about your feelings

Don't feel you have to make it all better. Just listening, validating feelings, and offering comfort is what your child needs from you. And be consistent—have snuggle time every night.

Our Family Can Shine

(Supplies: Yellow cardboard or construction paper, scissors, decorating supplies)

Your family has made it through a difficult time. There will be cloudy days when you may feel sad, angry, lonely, or other feelings of grief. And there will be sunny days when you feel happy, and can enjoy life. As times passes, the sunny days will happen more and more. It is good and healthy to let this sunshine into your lives and feel happy. Feeling happy, laughing and having fun does not mean that you have forgotten the person who died or that you don't still love him or her. Your family deserves to be happy and enjoy life. Today's art activity will help your family think and talk about the ways you can let sunshine into your lives and feel better. Cut out the sun on the next page, trace it onto yellow cardboard, and cut it out. Write each of the questions below in a separate ray on the sun. Discuss the questions together as a family, then write a response for each of the five questions (you can write your responses under each of the questions). Decorate the sun. Take the sun home, and put it on your fridge or somewhere you can all see it, so it will be a reminder that your family can, and deserves to shine!

2 things we learned about grief

A fun activity our family can enjoy together

Something new our family can try

Ways our family can help one another

Something that will make our family shine

Our Family Can Shine

Appendix A

Sample Graduation Letter
Below is a graduation letter written to a young client whose mother committed suicide:

Dear Cindy,

I am writing you this letter to let you know how proud I am of you! You have worked so hard in therapy and you have made wonderful progress. I remember when you first came to see me. You were only ten years old, and a terrible thing had recently happened in your life: your mother committed suicide. Like many grieving children, it was hard for you to talk about your mom's death. Even though you were so unhappy, you smiled a lot because you didn't want to face the sad feelings that you had inside. You had bad dreams and stomachaches a lot, and you felt guilty for your mom's suicide.

We did many activities together to help you talk about your feelings. You especially liked playing Feelings Tic-Tac-Toe because you got candy at the end of the games! You've come a long way in being able to express yourself, and that's great progress!

We played a lot of games together, but The Envelope Game stands out as one of the games that I think really helped you a lot. I remember when we played the game, we talked about how you blamed yourself for your mom's death, and how you wish you could have stopped her from killing herself. But your mom was so depressed that she was not thinking right. She could not see all the wonderful things in her life—like you! I'm glad The Envelope Game helped you to understand that your mom's death was not your fault. And the advice that you had for other grieving kids was very wise: Think about the good things in your life and you will feel better!

We spent many sessions talking about your mom, and all the special memories you have-- like outings to the zoo, going swimming, and baking cookies together. Even though your mom is dead, you can take comfort knowing that your special memories of her will last forever. When you miss your mom, you can listen to the memory tape you made, or cuddle up with the pillow you sewed from your mom's sweater, and this will help you feel closer to her.

Sometimes when you think about your mom, or when something good happens in your life and your mom isn't around to share the occasion, you may feel sad. It is normal and okay to cry and to let the sadness out! And, when you have happy times, it doesn't mean that you have forgotten your mom. You deserve to be happy and to enjoy life.

You have already been through a lot, but your experiences have made you a stronger person. You are a great kid; you are kind and thoughtful, you care about others, and you have a great sense of humor. You can be the kind of person your mom would be proud of.

Cindy, I have enjoyed working with you. You have done a great job sorting out your feelings, and talking about some very hard stuff. I wish you all the very best because you deserve it!
Yours Truly,
Liana Lowenstein

Appendix B

Treatment Plan for Bereaved Children

(Adapted from *The Child Psychotherapy Treatment Planner*, Jongsma & Peterson)

Individual and/or group therapy for the child to address the following:

Verbalize positive feelings toward the therapist

-Therapist to actively build the level of trust with the client through consistent eye contact, active listening, unconditional positive regard, and warm acceptance

-Therapist to explore, encourage, and support the child in verbally expressing feelings regarding the death

Verbalize and express a range of different feelings

-Complete the following interventions: Feeling Faces Cut N' Paste, Feelings Tic-Tac-Toe, Ali and Her Mixed-Up Feeling Jar

Verbalize increased awareness of normal feelings/reactions associated with grief

-Complete the following interventions: Shock and Denial, Feeling Scared and Worried, My Body Doesn't Feel Good, Getting Into Trouble, Heads or Tails Feelings Game

-Read books about grief (see list of books for bereaved children in resource section)

Implement adaptive coping techniques

-Use coping/self-soothing techniques through use of The Feel Better Bag

-Complete the following interventions: Feeling Lonely, Coping with Bad Dreams, Helping Myself When I Have Scary Thoughts, Feel Good Messages, Coping With Grief Game, Coping With Grief Attacks

Mourn the emotions associated with the death

-Complete the following interventions: My Story, Feeling Sad, Saying Goodbye

Verbalize anger and use appropriate techniques to cope with angry feelings

-Complete the following intervention: Feeling Angry

-Play Road Rage (from *More Creative Interventions for Troubled Children and Youth* by Lowenstein)

-Complete The Don't Flip Your Lid Anger Management Program (from *More Creative Interventions for Troubled Children and Youth* by Lowenstein)

Eliminate self-blame statements regarding the death

-Complete the following interventions: Feeling Like It's My Fault, Getting Rid of Guilt

Verbalize an understanding of death and an acceptance of the finality of the death

-Complete the following interventions: Life and Death, About Death, What Causes Death, What Happens After Death, I Wish My Special Person Was Still Alive, The Funeral, Basketball: A Game About Life and Death

Identify and preserve positive memories of the deceased
-Complete the following interventions: My Special Person, Memory Tape, A Penny for Your Thoughts, Keepsakes, Candle-lighting Ceremony
-Make a Pillow out of the deceased person's sweater

Increase positive thoughts about self and future
-Complete the following interventions: Making My Special Person Proud, Feeling Good About Myself, Wondering Why Bad Things Happen, Something Good Can Come From This, I Deserve To Be Happy

Express achievements in therapy and view termination as a positive process
-Complete the following interventions: What I Learned, Giving A Helping Hand, Looking At This Book
-Meet with caregiver(s) to prep for graduation ceremony and help them write letter to child for child's scrapbook
-Write a letter to child affirming achievements made in therapy
-Have a graduation ceremony

Therapy for child's caregivers and the family to address the following:

Caregiver to verbalize increased awareness of children's grieving process
-Read Handout for Caregivers
-Read books about bereaved children (see list of books for caregivers in resource section)

Increase open communication in the family about the death
-Complete the following interventions: Family Card Game, Postcards

Caregiver to create a safe and consistent environment
-Complete the following intervention: Nightly Snuggle

Participate in mourning rituals together as a family
-Complete the following interventions: Memory Book, Candle-Lighting Ceremony, Ways to Honor and Remember Our Loved One

Family to reorganize itself after the loss
-Complete the following intervention: Family Changes

Increase hope for healing
-Complete the following intervention: Our Family Can Shine

Appendix C

Information and Tips for School Personnel

This handout is designed to help you learn more about how children experience grief and what you can do as an adult working in the school setting to help children through this difficult time.

Grief is the word used to describe the intense emotional distress one experiences following a loss.

Important Points about Children and Grief

Children often show rather than talk about their grief. Their behavior, play, and interactions often reflect their grief.

Children grieve in small doses as they cannot tolerate prolonged periods of emotional pain. A child who is grieving may quickly shift from being sad to laughing and playing. This does not mean they don't care or are not grieving.

Some children may seem unaffected. They may not understand that death is permanent--that is, they may believe the person is coming back. Some children try to deny the reality of the death in order to avoid intense painful feelings. Others hide their sadness in an attempt to help caregivers feel better.

Children often blame themselves for the death. They may think their thoughts, wishes, or behavior made the person die.

Children usually don't tell you they are grieving. You can tell by what they say and do. No two children grieve the exact same way, but there are typical grief reactions that can help you know a child is grieving:

Behavioral reactions: Regressed or immature behavior (clinginess, thumb sucking, tantrums), overly mature (trying to replace dead parent's role), withdrawal, aggression, defiance, hyperactivity (often misdiagnosed as ADHD), easily startled or jumpy, hoarding foods or toys, perfectionism, re-enacting the death through play or artwork

Emotional reactions: Numbness, sadness, anger, guilt, fears, anxieties, hopelessness, loneliness, self-blaming, crying uncontrollably or not at all

Physical reactions: Stomachaches, headaches, overeating or under-eating, increased illnesses

Cognitive reactions: Difficulty concentrating, preoccupied with the loss, poor self-esteem

The above are normal reactions to loss. There is cause for concern if the reactions seriously interfere with the child's ability to function for a prolonged period of time.

How School Personnel Can Help Grieving Students

Inform others (teachers, school administration, school counselors/psychologists) and coordinate services. Inform school staff who may have contact with the child to make sure they know that the child has suffered a loss and may be experiencing difficulties or changes in school performance as a result. In this way, school staff can ensure that children get the support and understanding they need. Identify a safe, supportive individual at school the child can go to, and let the child know who he/she is.

Answer a child's questions. Let the child know you are available to talk about the death if he or she wants to. When talking to children about death, accept their feelings (even anger), listen carefully, and remind them that their reactions are normal. Use words that invite more, such as, "Can you tell me more about that", or "What was that like?" Do not force the child to talk about the death if s/he does not want to.

Maintain normal school routines as much as possible. Grieving children often feel their lives are chaotic and out of control, and need a regular routine and predictability. Balance normal school expectations with flexibility. If the child has fallen behind in his or her schoolwork, make a plan with the child and his or her caregivers to help him or her complete it. Provide extra help if needed, or a study buddy.

Give positive attention to the child. If the child is engaging in negative attention-seeking behavior, try to ignore this misbehavior and focus on the positive behavior. If the child is overly aggressive or oppositional, respond to the misbehavior by setting a limit, and giving an acceptable alternative, i.e. "It's not okay to throw your pencil on the floor. You can let out your frustration by squeezing your pencil." Do not punish the child by taking away recess; children need breaks and positive outlets for their energy. Try to **understand the meaning behind the behavior**. Usually, the child's behavior is communicating an unmet need, for instance, a need to be empowered, nurtured, praised, heard, respected, etc.

If the death occurred a while ago (even years ago), **don't expect the child to be "over it."** People do not stop grieving a significant death. While their grief lessens in intensity over time, painful feelings are triggered at certain times, such as the anniversary of the death date. Be sensitive to certain days that may be difficult for the child, i.e. if the death was a parent, then Mother's Day, Father's Day, or parent-teacher interviews may trigger painful feelings. Also, be aware that some children may grieve years later, when they have the emotional or developmental capacity to face painful feelings.

Reach out to the child's family. Be caring and supportive and make arrangements for ongoing communication about the child's progress and needs.

If the child's grief reactions are seriously interfering with his or her functioning, **consider a referral to a mental health professional, after clearing this with the child's caregiver.** Make sure the referral is to someone who has considerable experience working with children and with issues of grief and trauma.

Resources

Books for Children

When Dinosaurs Die: A Guide To Understanding Death by L. Krasny Brown, M. Brown

A Child's Book About Death by E. Grollman and J. Johnson

The Next Place by W. Hanson

Sam's Dad Died/Molly's Mom Died by M. Holmes

The Empty Place by R. Temes (sibling death)

Mick Harte Was Here by B. Park (sibling hit by truck)

Stacey Had A Little Sister by J. Friedman (sibling death)

When Your Grandparent Dies by V. Ryan

The Rainbow Feelings of Cancer by C. Martin

The Family Cancer Book by S. Rugg

Lost and Found: Remembering a Sister by E. Yeoman (sibling death from cancer)

Bart Speaks Out: Breaking the Silence on Suicide by L. Goldman

The Boy Who Sat By The Window by C. Loftis, C. Gallagher (homicide)

After A Murder by The Dougy Center

Love, Mark by M. Scrivanti (to order call 315-475-4673) (letters to children about grief)

I Know I Made It Happen by L. Bennett Blackburn (addresses feelings of guilt)

Tear Soup by P. Schwiebert and C. Deklyen

Tough Boris by M. Fox (gives permission for children to cry)

Brave Bart: A Story for Traumatized And Grieving Children by C. Sheppard

You Are Not Alone by B. Steele

Aarvy Aardvark Finds Hope by D. O'Toole (Storybook and Video)

Books for Caregivers

Talking About Death: A Dialogue Between Parent and Child by Earl Grollman

Helping Children Grieve & Grow by D. O'Toole

But I Didn't Say Goodbye by B. Rubel (Helping children cope with suicide)

What Parents Need To Know by B. Steele

References and Suggested Reading

Boyd-Webb, N. (1993) *Helping bereaved children: A handbook for practitioners.* New York: Guilford.

Burroughs, M.S., Wagner, W.W., & Johnson, J.T. (1997). Treatment with children of divorce: A comparison of two types of therapy. *Journal of Divorce and Remarriage, 27*(3-4), 83-99.

Cavert, C. (1999). *Games (& other stuff) for group.* Oklahoma City: Wood & Barnes Publishing.

Cohen, J. et al. (2001) *Cognitive-behavioral therapy for traumatic bereavement in children. Treatment manual.* Pittsburgh, PA: Center for Traumatic Stress in Children and Adolescents, Department of Psychiatry, Allegheny General Hospital.

Fink, R.S. (2002) What murder leaves behind: Special considerations in the treatment of surviving family members. In D.B. Bass and R. Yep (Eds.), *Terrorism, trauma, and tragedies: A counselors guide to preparing and responding.* Alexandria, Virginia: American Counseling Association.

Fogarty, J. (2000). *The magical thoughts of grieving children.* New York: Baywood Publishing Company

Gil, E. (1994). *Play in family therapy.* New York: Guilford.

Ginott, H. (1961). *Group psychotherapy with children: The theory and practice of play therapy.* New York: McGraw-Hill.

Jongsma, A. (2002). *The child psychotherapy treatment planner.* Hoboken, NJ: Wiley.

Kendall, P. (2000). *Childhood disorders.* East Sussex, UK: Psychology Press.

Lehmann, L, Jimerson, S, & Gaasch, A. (2001). *Mourning child grief support group curriculum.* Routledge.

Lieberman, A.F. Compton, N., Van Horn, P, & Ghosh Ippen, C. (2003). *Losing a parent to death in the early years: Guidelines for the treatment of traumatic bereavement in infancy and early childhood.* Washington DC: Zero to Three Press.

Lowenstein, L. (1995). The resolution scrapbook as an aid in the treatment of traumatized Children. *Child Welfare.* 74:4: 889-904.

Lowenstein, L. (1999). *Creative interventions for troubled children & youth.* Toronto, ON: Champion Press. (To order call: 416-575-7836 or www.lianalowenstein.com)

Lowenstein, L. (2002). *More creative interventions for troubled children & youth.* Toronto, ON: Champion Press. (To order call: 416-575-7836 or www.lianalowenstein.com)

McKissock, D. (2004). *Kid's grief: A handbook for group leaders.* Compassion Books.

Rohnke, K. and Butler, S. (1995). *Quicksilver.* Dubuque, Iowa: Kendall/Hunt Publishing Company.

Rugg, S. (2000). *Puppet plays for grieving children.* Rising Sun Center For Loss and Renewal.

Schaefer, Charles, E. (Ed). (2003). *Foundations of play therapy.* New Jersey: John Wiley & Sons, Inc.

Steele, B. (2003) *After a traumatic loss.* National Institute for Trauma and Loss.

Steele, B, Malchiodi. (2002) *Helping children feel safe.* National Institute for Trauma and Loss.

Sweeney, D. and Homeyer, L. (1999). *Group play therapy.* San Francisco: Jossey-Bass.

Utay, J.M., & Lampe, R.E. (1995). Use of group counseling game to enhance social skills of children with learning disabilities. *Journal for Specialists in Group Work, 20* (2), 114-120.

Walsh, F., & McGoldrick, M. (Eds.). (1991). *Living beyond loss: Death in the family.* New York: Norton.

Wolfelt, A. (1996). *Healing the bereaved child.* Companion Press.

Worden, W. (1996). *Children and grief.* New York: Guilford.

Organizations

Association for Death Education and Counseling: 847-509-0403; www.adec.org

American Academy of Bereavement: www.bereavementacademy.org

National Center for Death Education: www.mountida.edu

American Association of Suicidology: 303-692-0985

The Dougy Center: 503-775-5683; www.dougy.org

National Child Traumatic Stress Network: www.NCTSNet.org

National Institute for Trauma and Loss in Children: 877-306-5256; www.tlcinstitute.org

American Academy of Child and Adolescent Psychiatry: 202-966-7300; www.aacap.org

Center for Mental Health Services: 800-789-2647; www.mentalhealth.org

Association For Play Therapy: 559-252-2278; www.a4pt.org

Canadian Association For Child And Play Therapy: 800-361-3951; www.cacpt.com

The American Art Therapy Association: 847-949-6064; www.arttherapy.org

Canadian Art Therapy Association: www.catainfo.ca

Suppliers of Therapy Materials

Rising Sun Center for Loss and Renewal (grief resources): www.risingsuncenter.com

Oriental Trading Company (coffin, treasure chest, jungle animals, stickers): 800-875-8480

Anna's Toy Depot (mini tombstone, treasure chest, doll family): 888-227-9169

Rose Play Therapy (coffin, tombstone, treasure chest, jungle animals): 800-713-2252;

www.esticker.com (stickers)

About The Author

Liana Lowenstein, MSW, RSW, CPT-S, is a Registered Social Worker and Certified Play Therapy Supervisor in Toronto, Canada. She maintains a private practice specializing in assessing and treating children with a variety of emotional difficulties. In addition to her clinical work, she lectures internationally on child trauma and play therapy. She is on the teaching faculty of the Canadian Association for Child & Play Therapy, and she provides clinical supervision and consultation to mental health practitioners. She is author of numerous publications including the books, *Paper Dolls & Paper Airplanes: Therapeutic Exercises for Sexually Traumatized Children* (Crisci, Lay and Lowenstein, 1997), *Creative Interventions for Troubled Children & Youth* (1999), *More Creative Interventions for Troubled Children & Youth* (2002), and *Creative Interventions for Children of Divorce* (2006).

Innovative Child Therapy Books

Creative Interventions
for Troubled Children & Youth
Liana Lowenstein

This best-selling collection is filled with creative assessment and treatment interventions to help clients identify feelings, learn coping strategies, enhance social skills, and elevate self-esteem. Includes a special section on termination activities. A wealth of practical tools. For ages 4-16 in individual, group, and family therapy. Paperback, 128 pages.
US $25   CDN $30

MORE Creative Interventions
for Troubled Children & Youth
Liana Lowenstein

Presents MORE creative interventions to engage clients and help them address treatment issues such as feelings identification, anger management, social skills, and self-esteem. Includes techniques to manage challenging client behavior. A great sequel to Liana Lowenstein's last best-selling book. For ages 4-16 in individual, group, and family therapy. Paperback, 148 pages.
US $25   CDN $30

Paper Dolls and Paper Airplanes:
Therapeutic Exercises for Sexually Traumatized Children
Liana Lowenstein, Marilynn Lay, and Geraldine Crisci

A uniquely creative compilation of interventions to help bereaved children understand and express grief, diffuse traumatic reminders, address self-blame, commemorate the deceased, and learn coping strategies. Includes special activities for cancer, suicide, and homicide, and tips for caregivers and school personnel. For ages 7-12 in individual, group, and family therapy. Paperback, 205 pages.
US $35   CDN $40

Creative Interventions for
Bereaved Children
Liana Lowenstein

A uniquely creative compilation of interventions to help bereaved children understand and express grief, diffuse traumatic reminders, address self-blame, commemorate the deceased, and learn coping strategies. Includes special activities for cancer, suicide, and homicide, and tips for caregivers and school personnel. For ages 7-12 in individual, group, and family therapy. Paperback, 205 pages.
US $35   CDN $40

Creative Interventions for
Children of Divorce
Liana Lowenstein

An innovative collection of therapeutic games, art techniques, and stories to help children understand divorce, express feelings, deal with loyalty binds, disengage from parental conflict, address self-blame, and learn coping strategies. Includes tips for parents, and a ten-week group counseling curriculum. For ages 7-12 in individual, group, and family therapy. Paperback, 175 pages.
US $35   CDN $40

- -

Order Form
To order simply complete this form and mail with payment to the address below.

Name: _____ Agency: _____ Phone#: _____ Email: _____

Address: _____ City: _____ State/Prov: _____ Zip/PC: _____

Creative Interventions for Troubled Children & Youth : US $25 CDN $30 QTY_____
More Creative Interventions for Troubled Children & Youth : US $25 CDN $30 QTY_____
Paper Dolls and Paper Airplanes: Therapeutic Exercises for Sexually Traumatized Children : US $40 CDN $60 QTY_____
Creative Interventions for Bereaved Children: US $35 CDN $40 QTY_____
Creative Interventions for Children of Divorce: US $35 CDN $40 QTY_____

Shipping charges: Orders under $35.00 add $5.00, orders over $35.00 add 15% of total. Canadians add 6% GST on total. <u>All orders must be pre-paid.</u> Cash or check payable to Liana Lowenstein. Total enclosed: _____

Mail completed form with payment to:
Liana Lowenstein, Pharma Plus, PO Box 91012, 2901 Bayview Avenue, Toronto, ON M2K 1H0 Canada

For further information contact Liana Lowenstein: Tel: 416-575-7836 Email: liana@globalserve.net
Thank you for your order!